W9-BNI-646

Winners Are Not Those Who Never Fail But Those Who Never Quit

by

Edwin Louis Cole

ALBURY PUBLISHING
Tulsa, Oklahoma

Unless otherwise indicated, all Scripture quotations are taken from the *King James Version* of the Bible.

Some Scripture quotations marked AMP are taken from *The Amplified Bible. Old Testament* copyright © 1965, 1987 by Zondervan Corporation. *New Testament* copyright © 1958, 1987 by The Lockman Foundation. Used by permission.

Verses marked TLB are taken from *The Living Bible*, copyright © 1971. Used by permission of Tyndale House Publishers, Inc., Wheaton, Illinois. All rights reserved.

Scripture quotations marked NASB are taken from the *New American Standard Bible*. Copyright © The Lockman Foundation 1960, 1962, 1963, 1968, 1971, 1972, 1973, 1975, 1977. Used by permission.

Scripture quotations marked NKJV are taken from *The New King James Version* of the Bible. Copyright © 1979, 1980, 1982 by Thomas Nelson, Inc., Publishers. Used by permission.

3rd Printing

Winners Are Not Those Who Never Fail
But Those Who Never Quit
ISBN 1-57778-079-5
Facing the Challenge of Crisis and Change
ISBN 1-56292-112-6
Copyright © 1993 by Edwin Louis Cole
Christian Men's Network
International Communication Center
P. O. Box 10
Grapevine, Texas 76099-0010
USA
Published by ALBURY PUBLISHING
P. O. Box 470406
Tulsa, Oklahoma 74147-0406

Printed in the United States of America. All rights reserved under International Copyright Law. Contents and/or cover may not be reproduced in whole or in part in any form without the express written consent of the Publisher.

CONTENTS

Part I: The Crisis of Adversity

1   God Will Make a Way...9

2   God Will Be Faithful to You...............................15

3   God Will Speak to You..27

4   God Will Restore All 41

Part II: The Crisis of Change

5   God's Pattern for Change....................................51

6   Steps to Entering and Leaving 63

7   Mid-Life Crisis 85

8   The Way to Victory...91

Part III: Maintaining Victorious Living

9   How To Move From Failure to Success 99

10 The Power of Your Confession of Faith.........107

11 Speaking God's Words......................................115

ACKNOWLEDGEMENTS

I want to acknowledge the efforts of my daughter, Joann Webster, in not just assisting me in writing this book, but in facing the challenge of making sure I did it. Her indefatigable efforts made it possible.

PART I
THE CRISIS OF ADVERSITY

Chapter 1

GOD WILL MAKE A WAY

Crisis is generally the reason behind feelings of wanting to give up. In times of crisis we can be tempted to "chuck it all," "forget it," "give it up." Giving up and giving in during a crisis is one of the most demoralizing decisions we can make. Yet, facing the crisis, then overcoming it, can lead to our greatest success.

Crisis is the natural result of change which is one thing we can always be sure of. The world is in a constant state of flux. People's lives change, the business climate fluctuates, world powers realign, history marches on. The earth and our environment constantly evolve. Crisis results in and from change. Crisis includes such things as job changes, family conflicts, and social pressures. Both change and crisis are normal to life.

The crises we face both individually and corporately can lead us to a better life, or become degenerative. The outcome rests not in the nature of the issue but in what we do with the crisis. The agony of failure and tormenting thoughts of giving up are feelings shared by "winners" and "losers" alike. What people do with the situation is what separates the winners from the losers. *"Winners are not those who never fail, but those who never quit."*[1]

Pop psychologists today preach that people can control the outcome of their crises. "Take charge of your destiny" is their battle cry. In their theories, they give humans the dual responsibility of dealing with the crisis, and controlling the outcome.

They are half right. In reality, God charges each of us with the responsibility to conduct ourselves through times of change and crisis in a manner consistent with His Word and character. But He controls the outcome for us. We do our part; He does His part. The difference between what the world preaches and what God teaches is subtle, yet eternally significant.

This book offers three powerful tools that balance our responsibility with God's divinity: two to help us make it through any change or crisis; one to help us maintain the victory that we obtain. Take these truths, apply them to your life, and instead of just living from crisis to crisis you will begin to live according to God's Word, "from glory to glory."[2]

We never know when crisis will come. Someone once said, "You are either in a crisis, or about to be faced with one." Such is the normal ebb and flow of life.

Crisis is common in life.

Crisis is normal to life.

No one can live in this life without crisis.

Now that we understand that, let's see what can be done about it, how to handle it, where we can get help in it, and how we can make it a positive instead of a negative factor in life.

The stress that accompanies crisis is the factor that makes it seem so unbearable. A common desire for escape in people is the wish to return to ancient, more simple times or to earlier, less-pressured days of their lives.

However, our ancestors and forebearers did not experience less stress because their lives were less sophisticated, or because their modes of communication separated them from modern methods and the fast pace of our "fax" and "modem" world.

Adam and Eve, as recorded in Scripture, ran away from their denial of God's authority and attempted to hide from God. Their sin produced the stress of guilt, fear, and hiding.

Men and women, pioneers, who founded America, lived in privation as they sailed the seas, suffered from constant apprehension, danger, fear, and anxiety as they pressed on from

East to West founding the nation. In addition to the care and feeding of the family, they had the added pressure of forging a new nation economically, socially and politically.

History recounts the ordeals of the Donner party, who tried to reach California from the East. While en route they were faced with the wilderness weather of the Rockies. Trapped by winter in the almost impassable mountains they had to climb, unable to continue until the weather changed, the survivors resorted to cannibalism.

That is stress! That is living in crisis.

Since stress accompanies crisis, stress is as common to life as is crisis. A proper amount of stress, with its emotional, mental, and even physical pressure, is something to be accepted and even used as much as possible for positive good.

A certain amount of pressure is needed to fine-tune a guitar or piano, a business, and even a person. People are not exempt. It's necessary to healthy living. Fitness requires some stress.

Pressure that is not used properly, however, can become the source of disaster by snapping the musical string, causing a mental breakdown, and at times destroying the person as well as a business.

Stress can come from a variety of sources, either internal or external, within or without.

The Apostle Paul endured hardship while sailing to Rome aboard a prison ship. He told the captain the ship would be in danger from disaster if it left the harbor because the Lord had warned him of a storm coming up. Not believing the word of the Lord, and listening to other counsel, the captain ordered the crew to sail with Paul and other prisoners on board.

When the storm came, the ship was tossed for days on the high seas, and the sailors and passengers alike feared for their lives before the storm's fierceness. The constant, unrelenting gale caused apprehension, anxiety, and alarm over their fate.

Even though Paul was the victim of another's decision, he had

11

an anchor in his belief. He was strong in prayer while others were weak in panic. He rode out the storm on his knees. Though having to submit to another's poor decision, Paul was not discouraged, and finally heard the Lord tell him that if everyone would stay with the ship, they would all be saved. When Paul gave the captain the Lord's instruction, this time he listened, and ultimately they all made it safely to land.³

The captain acted in faith on his trust in Paul's word. Paul acted in faith on his trust in God's Word.

We may encounter people whose mistakes bring us hardship or loss, yet we, like Paul, also have an anchor to the soul — our faith in Christ. Like the captain, we may lose some ships in our lives, but if God is with us in the midst of the storm, we don't have to lose our lives for the sake of the ship.

When we reach the end of ourselves and think there is nothing left in us to face the circumstances of life; when we cannot see anything else that can be done to end the crisis; when there is no understanding of what to do or which way to turn; when our ship of finances, marriage, business, or ministry is going down and it seems is about to sink; when we seem to be alone, naked, stripped of everything; the good news is — *God is faithful!*⁴

God says that He is faithful to His children even when they seem to be totally depleted of faith. Even when our prayers ring hollow and seem to bounce back off the ceiling at us, He is faithful to us. We and God each have a different perspective of our lives. We see our life as a tapestry that on our side is filled with tangles and snarls, but He sees it from His perspective, the other side, which is the finely finished product.

God never fails.

God never quits.

God never ends anything on a negative.

God is faithful!

Remember

- Crisis is generally the reason behind feelings of wanting to give up.

- Crisis is the natural result of change.

- The crises we face both individually and corporately can lead us to a better life.

- Crisis is normal to life.

- The right amount of stress can be used to motivate us in positive ways.

Chapter 2
GOD WILL BE FAITHFUL TO YOU

Since God created the universe with His words, He has the power to stop it instantaneously with another word. If He can create or stop our entire universe with a word, how much more can He overcome any troubling situation in our lives.

Those who have experienced a personal relationship with God in Christ by repentance and faith, who have learned to trust Christ as Lord and Savior, can comprehend God's faithfulness, benefit from it, and understand His ability. Scripture says that men know there is a God by natural law.[1] Man's conscience, desire for timelessness, and capacity for loneliness, affirm the fact that inwardly all people have a natural desire for God where there is timelessness and unity with Him.

A common question of unbelievers is, "If there is a God, why does He allow war, birth defects, disease, etc.?" Since they know in their hearts that God must exist, what they are really asking is, "Why doesn't God use His power to stop or change things?"

Christians, however, believe that God has the power to do anything. Too often they have doubts, not about God's ability but His faithfulness. Their question is not, "Can He do it?" but "Will He do it for *me*?" In the weak state of their faith, they wonder, "Will He work on *my* behalf?"

Although many believers believe that God is *able*, they find it difficult to accept that He is *faithful*, and that He *will* act on their behalf. Unlike an unbeliever, we believe. But like the unbeliever, we don't often believe that He will work for *us*! When we don't

15

trust God to work in our behalf, we find it difficult to obey Him.

Scripture states that God is both *faithful* and *able*.[2] We must believe that God is faithful to help us.

The reason for wars, birth defects, disease, and other problems that plague humanity is that sin has caused them. They did not exist until sin came into the world. Because of what sin, selfishness, and Satan have done to human society, and the planet, God does for man what man cannot do for himself.

Through Christ, God provides a solution to the ills of the world. *The victory of the redeemed is not that they transform the world, but that they overcome the world by the transforming power of God's Spirit in them.* Through Christ, His Spirit resurrects us from death in trespasses and sins, and lifts us into a realm of faith above the world system and its iniquity.

People transpose the ills of society from self and Satan to God. Our problem is not that God is unfaithful, but that man is unfaithful. Transposition is a common error in man. A typical error is for writers to transpose words when typing, which alters meaning, transposes theory and practice. Such transpositions change unite to untie. One of the principles of the Kingdom of God is, "...commit...to *faithful* men, who shall be *able* to teach others also."[3] Too often this principle is transposed in practice by committing to *able* men, and then trying to make them *faithful*. In so doing, we not only pervert meaning, but frustrate the truth.

In transposition we try to find men of ability and then make them faithful. That is done by women in marriage, men in business, preachers in ministry, all with tragic results. It is unwise to trust an unfaithful man, regardless of his talent or ability. His talent cannot compensate for his lack of character.

Character undergirds talent.

Ability is built on talent and practice, but character is built on the cornerstone of faithfulness.

All around us we see the wreckage of lives, institutions, and businesses by talented, "able," but unfaithful men. On the other hand, everything of value has been built through someone's faithful efforts.

"Moreover it is required in stewards, that a man be found faithful," is how Scripture states it.[4]

Faithful men are the bedrock of the Church, the nation, and the world. God commits the leadership of His Church to faithful men.

Faithfulness means to be "firm in adherence to promises or in observance of duty." It also means, "true to the facts, to the standard, or to an original." Faithfulness is synonymous with words such as loyal, constant, staunch, steadfast, and resolute. It implies unswerving adherence; firm resistance to the temptation to betray; firmness of emotional attachment: fortitude and resolution; imperviousness to influences that would weaken it; steady and unwavering in love, allegiance or conviction; and determination to adhere to a cause or purpose.[5]

Faithfulness is a mark of maturity.

Constancy, loyalty, and strength are its evidence.

God requires men to be faithful.

The scriptural principle of promotion states that men must be "faithful in that which is least" before being promoted to places of authority that are greater.[6] The basic principle is:

Promote only what is proven.

My question is this: If men are required by God to be faithful, *what about God?*

In a world marred by errors, mistakes, transposition, where often the faithful man is ignored and the talented, though unfaithful, is lauded and applauded, we tend to forget there is a higher order, a faithfulness beyond our human experiences. It is simply: *"God is faithful."*[7]

All the qualities of faithfulness are found in His very Being. God doesn't act or feel faithful, He simply *is* faithful.

God in His faithful character manifests, reveals and shows His faithfulness in relationship with men.

When a man is faithful, he is accountable for whatever is entrusted to him. Because God is faithful, He can be trusted to account for those of us who are His children. Jesus said He would not lose any who were entrusted to Him.[8] That is His testimony of faithfulness, that He is willing to account for us.

God Is Unchanging and Trustworthy

God upholds "all things by the word of his power," and Jesus is that Word of His power.[9] Just as God is faithful to uphold the "law of gravity," so God is faithful to love and care for us as He promised. His faithfulness is the foundation of our trust.

God is without change in His very nature.[10] Although the world constantly changes, God never changes, wavers, or varies. When we are in the trying, volatile, difficult times that suffering, adversity, stress, and crisis produce, it is natural to think that everything around us is collapsing and that all is soon to be lost. Failure is a common result of effort.

God continues to uphold you and the universe. And God always will. He never wavers.

Whatever the cause of your crisis — job loss, marital tensions, mid-life frustration, religious or social persecution — you must remember that though outward appearances and inward emotions change, not everything has changed.

God is the same. God is faithful to His Word and to *you!*

God is said to be without "variableness" or "shadow of turning."[11] He never slumbers, sleeps, forgets,[12] falters, stumbles, reneges, or repents.[13] He is not a man that He should lie.[14]

God can be trusted totally.

Everything in human life varies. Weather, earth configurations, political entities, ideologies and philosophies, medicine and its practice, stock markets, and people all change. It has been said, "Everyone talks about the weather, but no one does anything about it."[15] As often as the weather changes, so might our emotions, circumstances, experiences, and relationships. They vary from moment to moment — but God never varies.[16]

God never varies.

In times of crisis when we are ridden by anxiety, depressed mentally, burdened with cares, steeped in stress, our greatest hope and comfort is knowing that God is faithful. His Word is our Rock,[17] our foundation for faith.

The foundation of a skyscraper is what sustains the superstructure in storms, earthquakes, and even bomb attacks. The superstructure doesn't hold itself together, it simply rests on the foundation. The foundation enables the building to stand steadfast.

Jesus is foundational for life.

He is the Rock, the Word, the Faithful One.

God Will Do It

"For as the rain cometh down, and the snow from heaven, and returneth not thither, but watereth the earth, and maketh it bring forth and bud, that it may give seed to the sower, and bread to the eater:

"So shall my word be that goeth forth out of my mouth: it shall not return unto me void, but it shall accomplish that which I please, and it shall prosper in the thing whereto I sent it."[18]

God and His Word remain the same regardless of us, who or what we are, or how we react to crisis. Whatever our state or condition, circumstance, or environment, God and His Word are

19

still the same. God is true to Himself and His righteous nature.

Because God is faithful to His Word, His Word will produce the results of His promises. When we apply the Word to our lives, we can expect the results of His promises. God's promises are trustworthy. His Word is true and faithful.

To trust in that which is not truth is to trust in a lie. We can give ourselves totally to Jesus and completely rely upon His Word because He is Truth. Jesus is total Truth, therefore He is totally trustworthy.

In the throes of crisis it is not uncommon to find our thoughts revolve only around our own problem. Days and nights are consumed with "our situation." At times when we think we are worrying about ourselves, we are really worrying about God.

Our worries are in many forms: "Will God come through for me in this one?" "I give up, I can't do anything but pray." "I've prayed, and I can't see any difference."

Worries center on self. Faith centers on God.

In our self-consumed attitude we must not think that after upholding the entire universe by His Word, God will let go of us.

Consumed with worry, we look at things from a purely earthly and natural perspective. We don't realize that when we doubt the outcome after placing it in God's hands, we are casting the shadow of doubt on God's very character. We are in essence thinking that God does not have a good enough character to keep His Word and maintain His vigilant care.

We must realize that our perspective is not God's. Ours is based on what we see naturally. We don't understand as God understands,[19] which is the reason we must act by faith.

"For we walk by faith, not by sight."[20]

We need to gain God's perspective. When we tear ourselves away from our own thoughts, perceptions, imaginings, and fears to focus on God's Word, we begin to see from His heavenly perspective and not our limited, earthly view. This is why reading God's Word is so vital.

We must read and feed on His Word.

Do it in the times of contentment and ease to prepare for the times of adversity.

A verse in Proverbs says, "You are a poor specimen if you can't stand the pressure of adversity."[21]

The ability to withstand adversity comes from faith. Faith comes from studying the Word of God and developing a Christlike character.

It is essential that between the times of crisis, as well as in it, we school ourselves to make the Word of God our ground of faith.

When a person repents and receives Jesus Christ as Lord, the Spirit brings the nature of God into the life by His indwelling power. The very life of Christ begins to inhabit the person. As the new believer spends time in God's Word, learns what God has revealed of Himself, the income of His thoughts is the outcome of a new life, filled with God's very own character.

The Spirit of holiness will only produce what is holy. As we imbibe the Spirit of God, we begin to make decisions not based on obligation to the laws of God, but emanating from the flow of God's Spirit in the innermost to the outermost areas of life.

When the believer encounters adversity, the Spirit of God does not leave, but continues to work faithfully within for the person's highest good. In all negative situations, regardless of the nature or source, God in His faithfulness never stops working for our good. As the Apostle Paul reminds us, "...we know that all that happens to us is working for our good if we love God and are fitting into his plans [for us]."[22]

You can trust God.

You can trust God to do right.

You can trust God to do right at all times.

You can trust God's Word.

You can trust God to be faithful to you.

You don't need to worry about God!

God Will Not Disown You

"It is a faithful saying: For if we be dead with him, we shall also live with him: if we suffer, we shall also reign with him...if we believe not, yet he abideth faithful: *he cannot deny himself.*"[23]

The paraphrase of the last verse of this passage reads:

"Even when we are too weak to have any faith left, he remains faithful to us and will help us, *for he cannot disown us who are part of himself,* and he will always carry out his promises to us."[24]

And *The Amplified Bible* translates it:

"If we are faithless (do not believe and are untrue to Him), *He remains true* [faithful to His Word and His righteous character], *for He cannot deny Himself.*"[25]

God always works for our good.

In the midst of our greatest crisis, His Transcendent Glory is to take what was meant for evil and turn it around and make it work for our good. We may not be able to see any good in what is happening, but God never stops working for our good. His Spirit has not departed from us, He has not rejected us, He has not turned His face away from us.

"He remains faithful" and "He cannot deny Himself." If the Spirit of God is in us by saving grace through Jesus Christ; and His nature and righteousness have been imparted to us by faith; and if we are identified with Him by Word, blood, and Spirit — then when we go through trying times, God will not deny us because for Him to do so would be to deny Himself.

God is not going to deny us because to deny us would be to deny Himself.

God is the source of salvation from death to eternal life, and He is the source of salvation from our problems to the "abundant life" Jesus promised us.

God Is the Source of Success

The Bible says, "A man may ruin his chances by his own foolishness and then blame it on the Lord!"[26] This means that some men make mistakes, create their own tragedies out of their own folly, then blame the results of their own failures and losses on God.

God is not a scapegoat for failure.

God is the source of our successes.

To make God the scapegoat for our failures is to eliminate His ability to be the source of our solutions.

God never fails.

To accuse God of failure is to accuse Him of not being God.

King David in the Old Testament experienced the worst defeat of his life when he camped at Ziklag with his band of armed men before rising to the throne of Israel. While he and his men were out of the camp, raiders came and carried off their goods and families. When the men returned, they were angry to the point of revolt. They talked of stoning David. We'll see David's response in Chapter 4, but consider the response of the men.

They followed David because they believed he was anointed by God to be king and they were sure to serve in his kingdom when he rose to the throne eventually. They aspired to high military and even political positions. They knew God's hand was on David, and by following David, they were in a sense following

23

after God. That's why they were drawn to David — he was God's man. Yet in crisis they talked of killing him.

They talked of killing the one they knew heard from God, the one who was being led by God in spite of his mistakes. In thinking this way, they were tempted to cut off their only hope of victory. Only God answering David's prayers kept them from their error. By following David through their crisis, they recaptured their families, recovered their losses, plus gained the bonus of the plunder from their enemies who were destroyed.

In a moment of extreme tension, mourning their loss and plight, inundated by the emotions experienced, listening to others' complaints and the growing indictment against David's leadership, they almost lost all. In their willingness to trust David, to "follow the leader," or, like Paul's crew, "stay with the ship," they not only experienced God's miracle and prosperity, but fulfilled their goals and achieved their dreams.[27]

Satan is an accuser,[28] deceiver, tempter, and liar.

Satan accuses God to men and men to God.

With his deceitful nature he bases his lies on half-truths.

Eve was seduced this way in Eden. Job suffered from Satan's deception.

The voice of Satan will tell you that God is unfaithful, that God is the source of your problems. You may be tempted to become mad at God and to believe that it is God Who has plagued you and is now going to abandon you to your own disaster. Satan is a liar, and the father of lies.[29] It is Satan's intention to convince you that God is not working for your highest good, to steal your faith, rupture your relationship with God, and destroy your life.

Satan will attempt to get you to fault or curse God, and by so doing cut off your only source of escape, avenue of victory, and road to success. Don't be deceived.

Failure can be the womb of success.

It is utter folly to accuse God of being the source of your hurt and harm and failure. God is the source of your success — not of your failure.

God is the genesis of every good thing in your life.

The patriarch Joseph as a young boy had a dream that enraged his brothers with jealousy. They sold him "down the river" into slavery. Years later when they experienced a severe famine, they appealed to Egypt for food. There they found Joseph free, safe, and secure in a position as second in command over the country. Shocked and afraid of him because of their misdeed years before, they tried to make amends. To calm them, Joseph uttered the pivotal phrase, "You meant it to me for evil, but God meant it to me for good."[30]

Others may mean evil, but when you submit it to God, His Transcendent Glory will turn it around for good.

Before going further, let's pause here and consider our own lives — your life. Are you in a position for God to be faithful to you? Are you His child? Have you been made alive in your spirit through the resurrection power of Jesus Christ? Are you identified with Him by His Word, blood, and the indwelling of His Spirit?

If you realize this is what you need, and you do not yet know Him, then pray and ask Him to forgive you and help you.

As you make Jesus the Lord of your life, by faith, God will use His resources on your behalf — His Transcendent Glory to take things meant for evil and make them work for good.

Remember

- Character undergirds talent.
- Faithfulness is a mark of maturity.
- Promote only what is proven.

- God can be trusted totally.

- God never varies.

- God is faithful even when we are faithless.

- Worries center on self; faith centers on God.

- We must read and feed on God's Word.

- Failure can be the womb of success.

- Trust is extended to the limit of truth. Jesus is complete Truth, so He can be trusted completely.

- We need God's perspective.

- The income of God's Word is the outcome of a changed life.

- God is always working for our highest good.

- God is the source of our success, the genesis of every good thing.

- God takes what is meant for evil and makes it work for our good.

Chapter 3

GOD WILL SPEAK TO YOU

Elijah was a man. A real man. God's man. Rugged, individualistic, stalwart, a leader and loner. But then leadership can be a lonely life.

He was also a prophet. A man of conviction.

Along with Moses, he was and is one of God's greatest prophets, unique in the Kingdom of God. His spirit was to be the forerunner to Christ, and was found in the message of John the Baptist.

At times he suffered from persecution, betrayal, and denial, but he never lost his concern for God's honor and, in spite of people's opposition to his message, displayed great compassion for others.

Having suffered from religious persecution, personal rejection, and false blame for environmental drought and famine, he was no stranger to adversity and the stress it brings. But Elijah had a source of strength that few know — he was a man who could move the arm of God in prayer.

He prayed that it would not rain, and it didn't rain for three and a half years; then when he prayed again it began.[1] He moved the arm of God through prayers that God Himself authored. God showed His glory through the life of Elijah.

Elijah was not only a man of prayer, but was man's answer to prayer.

Elijah brought glory to God by his obedience, his dependence upon God, and his willingness to lose his life for God's sake. In his testing times, Elijah showed his character.

He faced times of adversity with self-control, but on one occasion experienced a crisis that almost took his life, and in it the fivefold temptations so common to crisis. They are:

Depression.

Despair.

Resignation.

Failure.

Inferiority.

The Bible says that Elijah "was a man subject to like passions as we are."[2] He was as human as any of us, faced his temptation with the same conflicts that we experience, and in desperation was brought to the brink of failure.

When we read the account of his trials, temptings, and testing we find that his greatest crisis did not come from external foes or the formidable circumstances he faced, but was within his own soul in his time of solitude.

Elijah's greatest battle came immediately after he achieved his greatest victory. King David yielded to temptation the day after one of his greatest victories. The Lord Jesus Christ was engaged by Satan in a battle of temptation immediately after being baptized with the Holy Spirit in the river Jordan.

There is a pattern and principle following great victories throughout Scripture and history, right up to the present time:

The day after the battle is more important than the eve.

The evening before battle is filled with the activity of preparation; plans to review, personnel to rehearse, mental reconsiderations, corrections to be made, weapons to be checked, and everything to be set in readiness. Then the battle is waged, and afterward the mental, emotional, and physical letdown comes.

It is the day after, when we are wearied, unarmed, and relaxed that we become most vulnerable. Our vigilance has diminished, we are not on-guard as before, and can be careless.

Noah experienced this after working for more than a century to prepare for the earth's flood, rescuing his family in the ark, and defeating unbelieving humanity outside the ark by the flood's destruction. Noah trusted God implicitly and was saved by faith.

However, after reaching high ground he relaxed, planted a vineyard, and drank of the vine — becoming drunk. In his indiscretion, one of his sons he had labored so long and hard to save, brought a curse upon himself. In the aftermath of Noah's greatest triumph he experienced his greatest defeat.[3]

Elijah Believes the Bad News

Elijah's path to victory and the ensuing crisis began when God directed him to pray for a drought on the land. A famine-producing drought was God's way of getting Israel's attention. Circumstances are one of the ways God deals with His people, and financial impoverishment is a crucial circumstance in any life.

Ahab, the ruling king in Israel at the time, was himself wicked and wickedly inspired by his evil wife, Jezebel. She advocated and spread the worship of the false god, Baal. Although Ahab disavowed the Lord God, when the drought came, he knew only Elijah had the knowledge of God that could forestall or end such a plague on the land.

Search parties discovered Elijah and arranged a confrontation between the king and the prophet. Ahab arrogantly demanded of Elijah, "Are you the one who is troubling Israel?"[4]

"What do you mean, am I the one who is troubling Israel?" Elijah asked incredulously. "You're the one who's causing all the trouble. You're the one who violated God's commandment not to have any gods before Him, and brought in all the idols. You're the problem, not me! I'm just trying to bring the solution."[5]

Ahab's perspective was typically human. He saw only the

drought — the consequences of his sin — and not the source of the problem — the sin itself.

To Ahab, Elijah was to blame because he prayed for the drought. By blaming God's prophet, Ahab was in reality blaming God for the plight of the nation.

This type of confrontation is similar to the continuing crises in nations of the world today. Those in our society who have wrought havoc and chaos with their ungodly philosophies and deeds stand in accusation against God's agents for trying to make right the wrong. No wonder the righteous suffer when the wicked rule.[6]

God's Word declares that He hates "those who say that bad is good, and good is bad."[7]

Perversion in society is at its worst when those who love evil find fault with those who love truth, and protect the perpetrators of error, sin, and wickedness by condemning those who contend for truth, righteousness, and godly principles.

Ahab maintained his innocence in regard to the drought, refused to accept the truth of Elijah's statements, and closed his mind to any thought that there could be some truth to Elijah's words. The conflict caused Elijah to issue a challenge to determine who is the true God — Baal the idol, or Jehovah the Lord God.

Elijah knew that Jezebel and Ahab supported the 450 prophets of Baal in Israel, keeping them on "state payrolls," to provide for the practice of their false religion. Infuriated with Elijah, motivated by their pride and arrogance, Jezebel and Ahab assigned their entire group of false priests to the contest with Elijah on Mount Carmel. Knowing in his heart the power of God in the life of Elijah, Ahab nonetheless sent his prophets to the mount hoping they would defeat God's prophet.

The nation of Israel awaited the outcome, for the honor of Jehovah God was at issue.

Elijah and the prophets of Baal each prepared altars, and each agreed to pray. Whichever god answered by fire would be acknowledged as the one true God. Out of the insane logic of the prophets of Baal, to cut down a tree and use one-half for an idol and the other for firewood, they created a god from their imaginations.[8] Deluded and deceived, they could not acknowledge its stupidity, though God's prophets tried to tell them how absurd their worship was.

Creating gods from their imaginations, and initiating equally imaginative ceremonies and "sacred" rites, false prophets are really worshippers of themselves. They follow the same perversion that caused Lucifer's expulsion from heaven, and ultimately to be known as Satan — the worship of self.

Despite all attempts and appeals to their god, Baal, nothing happened. Elijah began to ridicule their pathetic and powerless efforts with all their ranting and chanting.

When the time came for Elijah to prove his God, it was the hour of prayer for the Israelites, an habitual hour of power in his life. To demonstrate his faith in God before the people and prophets of Baal, he called for the sacrifice to be watered until the trench surrounding it was even filled. There would be no chance of manipulating the results.

When Elijah prayed, fire came down from heaven with such intense heat and light that it consumed not only the sacrifice but the water surrounding it, the very stones of the altar, and even scorched the ground where it had stood. Elijah knew by experience that "our God is a consuming fire."[9]

As the fire fell, the shouts of praise at the presence of God went up from the people. They cried in unison, "The Lord, he is God!"[10] Elijah seized the moment and ordered the people who were on the Lord's side to rid themselves of the false prophets of Baal, and so the people destroyed the idols, altars, and prophets. *There would be victory in the valley because there was glory on the mount.*

Elijah advised Ahab he was going to pray for rain, and advised him to leave Mount Carmel immediately. After Elijah prayed seven times, a cloud the size of a man's hand appeared out of the sea, and immediately became a storm that brought "a great rain."[11]

Upon his return to his palace, Ahab related how the prophets of Baal were all dead because of Elijah. In so telling he made Elijah to be a culprit in the eyes of Jezebel. Ahab's cowardice in the presence of his wife was caused by the vicious violence of her nature. He cowered at the thought of becoming the object of her wrath, and knowing his wife's infamous desire for vengeance, he painted a picture that so enraged her she sought to kill Elijah. This would secure what Ahab wanted but spare him the consequences of doing it himself. Wickedness and cowardice are related.

Jezebel threatened to kill Elijah. She sent a messenger to tell Elijah she would "have his head" by that same time the next day.[12]

Her threat to kill Elijah came when he was exhausted in body and spirit from his intense efforts and struggles in the battle against both his and the Lord's enemies. In his tired and weakened condition, the great prophet, the man of God who had just won a powerful victory in front of an entire nation, fell prey to sudden fear and overwhelming despair.

He was discovering the truth that if Satan cannot gain an advantage by temptation, he will try to defeat by accusation. When Satan could not overtake Elijah by either temptation or accusation, he tried intimidation. Elijah was suffering all three from the antichrist spirit in Jezebel — the "spirit of the spoiler." This same spirit was in Potiphar's wife when she tried to seduce and tempt Joseph in an earlier day.[13] To keep Joseph from rising to the greatness God intended for him, the spoiler tried to ruin him. It failed.

The spirit of antichrist is Satan's spirit, one that pits himself against God and everything godly. It is a spirit that attempts to make dirty those who are pure, to make cowards of those who show courage, to cause to bend or bow those who stand up for God.

It is a spirit which the Spirit of God overcomes.

The Fivefold Temptations

From the victorious and mighty contest and conquest of Mount Carmel, Elijah ran to escape from the threat of a lone woman. He ran figuratively and literally.

Wearied physically with his run of sixty miles from Mount Carmel, worn in spirit from the conflict with evil in both prophet and prophetess, he finally sat down under a juniper tree for rest and comfort. Gone was the glory of the revelation on Mount Carmel. Absent were the cries and cheers of the crowd which had stood with him. Behind him was the elation of winning the battle against all the evil forces in Israel. Worn and weary, he collapsed into temptation.

"It is enough; now, O Lord, take away my life; for I am not better than my fathers,"[14] he cried out to God.

In that one cry he showed he was facing the fivefold temptations of depression, despair, resignation, failure, and inferiority.

He was depleted physically, drained emotionally, depressed mentally, despairing spiritually — his desire to fight was gone — he was ready to give up and give in. But God was faithful.

As God's messenger, His moral agent in the world, Elijah had been given a powerful prophetic gift, and regardless of his emotional straits, God was not going to recall that gift. The whole world identified Elijah with God, as a prophet who did exploits in His Name. For God to deny Elijah would have been to deny Himself.

According to the Bible, the gifts and callings of God are "without repentance."[15] *The Living Bible* puts it this way: "For God's gifts and his call can never be withdrawn; he will never go back on his promises."[16]

God did not give up on Elijah even when Elijah wanted to give up on himself.

God did not leave Elijah alone.

Despite Elijah's depressed condition, wavering resolve, and

33

shattered morale, God would not forsake Elijah. Neither will God deny or forsake us in our weaknesses. God will not deny us, for He will not deny Himself. Think of it!

God is faithful.

To His Word, to His character, *to us.*

God did three things for Elijah.

God fed him.

God rested him.

God gave him quietness.

For recovery Elijah needed three things: rest, diet, and quiet.

In days of intensity and crisis, when life becomes too subjective, perspective too muddled, thinking too incoherent, and the need to know and understand too difficult, God will "provide a way of escape." It's an escape from ourselves to God.

A peaceful atmosphere creates a meditative spirit.

Even Jesus "went apart" for a season.[17] When you think of the ministry Jesus had — the anointing He carried, the demands people placed upon Him, the persecution against Him, the challenge to His character — you begin to realize the enormity of the pressure He was under.

He took time to be alone with the Father.

If Jesus and Elijah needed it — think how much more we do.

Elijah needed to hear from God. To do so he needed to be in a proper spiritual condition to hear that "still small voice."[18]

God waited to speak until Elijah was ready to hear.

Prepare To Hear From God

Wallowing in self-pity, consumed with his situation, his thoughts turned only inward, Elijah's perceptions became unclear.

His perception was based on deception. Seeing only his circumstances, he was sinking in a sea of self-pity — not unlike Peter who began to sink in a sea of water when he took his eyes off Jesus.

God knew there were seven thousand who had not bowed the knee in worship to Baal, though Elijah felt lonely and isolated. However, once rested and refreshed, Elijah began another journey to another mount, where he would hear the voice of God.

God spoke to Elijah in a "gentle whisper."[19] In quietness he again possessed his soul, heard from God, and became ready to receive the new revelation which would change and multiply his ministry.

God will do the same for us today.

The basic art of communication is the ability to hear.

It wasn't until Elijah stopped feeling sorry for himself, was rested in his mind and spirit, that God spoke to him. It would do no good for God to try to talk to Elijah while he was still speaking because Elijah wouldn't be able to hear what was said. When Elijah was ready to hear, God spoke. God's Word brought life and health, enabling Elijah to arise and continue in ministry.

The beauty of the relationship between God and Elijah was not just in Elijah's willingness to be identified with God, but in God's willingness to be identified with Elijah — both on the mount and under the juniper tree. God would simply not let go of His prophet.

Under God's direction, Elijah left the mount and found Elisha, tutored and schooled him in the ways of faith, and eventually left the mantle of ministry with him. The spiritual tides in Israel changed and Ahab and Jezebel died the dishonorable deaths due them. Elijah, a man who once desired to die under a juniper tree, ended his life without tasting death on this earth.

Instead, when God's purposes for Elijah were accomplished, *Elijah exchanged his juniper tree for a chariot of fire*, that ushered him into heaven.[20]

The turning point for Elijah was that in the midst of his aloneness, facing his most trying temptations, Elijah was able to hear God's voice. Once he heard, he obeyed. The path to deliverance starts when God reaches out to us, and continues when we obey Him. Whether or not we experience a turning point in our lives when God reaches out to us depends on our obedience to His Word.

God's power is released in our lives to the degree of our obedience, and no more.

Obedience is not based on emotion, but on faith. Faith is always the key element in obedience.

When Elijah obeyed God's Word, his emotions changed.

The principle is: *Emotions follow actions.*

Righteousness means "right standing" before God. There is no emotional quality to righteousness. It is a state of being. However, when the righteousness of Christ is imparted, the result is peace and joy, both of which have powerful emotional qualities in them.

Like righteousness, obedience and faith have no emotional qualities, but they have the ability to change a person's emotions.

In other words, *to change your emotions, change your actions.*

Obedience is an act of faith. Faith is belief in action. Belief is not faith until it is acted upon.

Faith is like wind — *it cannot be seen, only its results.*

Obedience is God's method of protection for our lives.

Living within His will, Word, and way is a life of obedient faith.

When Elijah acted obediently on what God said, his future became secure.

God's "Transcendent Glory" will take what is meant for harm and make it work for our ultimate good. God will take our most difficult times and make them work for our ultimate good when they are committed and submitted to Him.

God's "ultimate good" for our lives is "Christlikeness."

Living It

In a magazine article I mentioned Elijah and his juniper tree. A man who read it wrote to say that he suddenly realized he had been sitting under his own juniper tree for eight months since his wife died. Another wrote and said he had been fighting his fivefold temptations for three months since being fired from his job.

Rejection is the hardest thing in life for a man to take.

It was not just Jezebel's threat of physical harm that made Elijah run, but also the rejection he felt. Rejection caused dejection.

Under his juniper tree, facing his fivefold temptations, Elijah finally realized that God had not rejected him, only God's enemies. God had never stopped working for Elijah's good.

God never stops working for your good!

God brought Israel out of Egypt to take them into Canaan. God only brings you out in order to take you in. From the lesser to the greater. *Crisis is only the means of exchange.*

In Oklahoma City, I met a man who told me of his own personal experience.

Jerry was a missionary — married, two children — and in the midst of a major crisis in his life. His wife told him her love for him was gone. They could not communicate properly or civilly. He finally admitted to himself they were only together for the children's and ministry's sake, but his marriage was basically dead.

He was wallowing in his fivefold temptations.

The choice before him was to live out the lie of a loveless marriage, or lose both family and ministry. Knowing the traumatic

37

and dramatic changes either choice would force upon him, he earnestly sought God.

Late one night while reading his Bible, Jerry sensed the "still small voice" of the Lord in the scriptural command to "love your wife."[21] Jerry argued with the voice, stating he had tried being a loving husband. Only to have a second impression of that "still small voice" saying, "You haven't loved her as I told you to love her."

For days afterward Jerry mulled over the words.

Eventually realizing it was the Spirit of God, he began to meditate on what was meant. To "love her as Christ loves the Church" became another word from the Bible that came alive in his spirit.[22] Jerry decided that whatever that meant, he would endeavor to do it.

His first opportunity came two weeks later.

Every evening, in the middle of the night, their new child cried for the night-time feeding. Usually Jerry would pretend to sleep as his wife rose to meet the baby's needs. This night though, Jerry had a sudden thought bolt through his mind as he rolled over to try to sleep. He acted quickly, arising to tell his wife to go to sleep, he would take care of the baby.

As he fed the child, a new emotion took hold of Jerry, and a new appreciation for both mother and child rose in him.

He began to learn that *love is the desire to benefit others even at the expense of self, because love desires to give.* Love centers in the will, not the emotions.

As Jerry continued to look for other ways to help his wife, doing what he considered to be "loving," he began to discover he was falling in love all over again.

Jerry's wife noticed his changed behavior immediately and wondered about it. As it continued and even increased, she began to respond with acts of love in return. Over a period of months, Jerry and his wife experienced a marvelous transformation in their relationship.

Jerry obeyed when God spoke.

God never stopped working in their behalf.

Jerry's family received the benefit, Jerry had the blessing.

Jerry or Elijah — the principle is the same.

Remember

- The day after the battle is more important than the eve.

- If Satan cannot overcome a person by temptation, he'll try accusation, or intimidation.

- The fivefold temptations during crisis are: depression, despair, resignation, failure, and inferiority.

- The basic art of communication is the ability to hear.

- God brings us to a place of obedience before He speaks.

- God's power is released in life to the degree of obedience.

- Emotions follow actions.

- To change your emotions, change your actions.

- Crisis is only the means of exchange.

- Love is the desire to benefit others even at the expense of self, because loves desires to give.

- God never stops working for your good.

Chapter 4

GOD WILL RESTORE ALL

King David of Israel learned by experience the "fivefold temptations" men face in crisis.

Samuel the prophet anointed David to be king after Saul disobeyed God and disqualified himself for the position, yet Saul was still on the throne.

The period after his anointing, and prior to his rise to the throne, was a learning and proving time for David. It was God's testing time to prepare David for a long and prosperous reign. Saul discovered God's choice of David to succeed him, and in paranoid jealousy endeavored to kill David. Evading Saul and his mad attempts to murder him, David and his four hundred men took whatever course they could to stay alive.

While successfully avoiding Saul, David became tired. In a weak moment his faith in God gave way to a fear of Saul. David thought he would escape from Saul's assassins by moving into the land of the Philistines.

Bad Idea. In a weak moment, David made a decision to seek neutral territory. He would discover that in this life there is no neutral land. His decision came during a time of great stress, anxiety for his family and followers, out-and-out weariness, and it would prove to be a "degenerative decision."

Decisions determine destiny.

David would soon descend to the lowest point of his life.

David's decision was based on human wisdom, not God's promise, revelation, nor faith in either. It was a choice made while suffering from frustration. (Little wonder centuries later another prophet would write, "Be not weary in well doing."[1])

David compromised his position, and in doing so he compromised the people who depended on him.

Once David compromised in one area of life, this upright and godly leader began to compromise in other areas. David soon lied, committed fraud, and deceived the Philistine who trusted him.

Achish was a Philistine, living in Gath. David convinced Achish he was on his side and would serve him. Achish gave David and his men the benefit of his protection and friendship. But David carried out ruthless raids against other Philistine cities, killing, plundering, then reporting to Achish the raids were against enemies of Gath.[2]

David's decision took him away from God's will, but not out of God's reach.

God is a merciful God.

When David and his men left their home in Ziklag one day to go raiding again — enemies raided David. They took the best possessions of David and his men, kidnapped their families, and destroyed the town. When David and his men returned home they found only ashes and rubble.

In their grief and rage, David's men turned on him with murder on their minds. They had hoped to gain everything by following him, but instead had lost it all.

In that moment David faced the reality of his wrong decision and its consequences. It had brought him devastation and desolation, as all degenerative decisions do. David realized that his only hope, his only salvation, was in turning to God in total dependence upon His grace, mercy, and favor.

David's response to the disaster was to repent. Then he "encouraged and strengthened himself in the Lord his God."[3] This was why he was a man after God's own heart. He made mistakes — big ones — but he didn't look for ways to avoid reality. He confronted his mistakes in truth.

He encouraged himself by recounting what God had done in his life in other times of crisis when he called upon God, such as when Goliath fell before his rocks of faith. He recalled the promises, Scriptures, and revelations God had given him, and in those he found strength.

Then he prayed.

Prayer is what he had not done when he decided to go to seek neutral ground to escape from Saul.

Prayerlessness is often a form of hiding.

David sought God's counsel and guidance. Inquiring of God as to whether he should pursue the troop that had trashed his town, he asked God if he should "overtake them."[4]

When David was ready to hear, God spoke.

Being instructed of the Lord to pursue, and sure that he would overtake the troop and recover all, David led his men in pursuit of the raiders. As a result we read that "David recovered all that the Amalekites had taken...."[5]

When David recovered spiritually he was able to recover everything materially.

God was faithful.

God never left David.

Even while David was suffering the consequences of his compromise, God was setting in motion all the necessary elements that would clear the pathway to the throne for David. While David was occupied in recovering his spiritual balance in the battle of his life, King Saul was killed during a battle of his own. Ironically, at the same time Saul was killed through a compromise in battle to avoid harm, David recovered from his compromise to avoid harm from Saul.

God was faithful to bring David through his fivefold temptations, forgive him, provide him a way out, and still bring him to the place God intended for him to occupy.

Hold On — God *Is* Working

King David almost missed God's promise, Israel's throne, and his place in the lineage of Christ through impatience. By his decision to compromise and settle for "good," he almost lost God's best.

Impatience is a costly vice.

Impatience is a facet of unbelief.

Unbelief is the basis for sin.

The "prodigal son" in the parable of Jesus was impatient to gain his inheritance, and because he wasn't mature or responsible enough to take care of it, he squandered it.[6]

Men pay the highest cost for the lowest living.

More men miss God's answers to prayers, fulfillment of dreams, and realization of hopes, through impatience than through anything else.

There is no impatience in God.

Some people don't pray long enough, believe long enough, trust long enough, hold on long enough, or wait long enough, and lose instead of win.

I cannot count the times I have received a letter from some desperate man asking for prayer because of some crisis, only to receive a jubilant letter a few months later from the same man saying, "You won't believe what happened to me!"

Yes! I will believe it!

"Praise is comely for the upright,"[7] is what Scripture says.

Believers have a right to praise God in the midst of crisis and temptation, because at that moment, by faith, they know God is working for their good.

When it appeared the entire crew on board the ship with Paul would be lost, in the midst of the storm, when all seemed pointless, Paul told the crew to be of "good cheer," none would be lost.[8]

When the ship sank and they came to land, Paul and his men were hosted by a company of people. Out of the fire that was built on the beach came a poisonous snake that bit Paul.[9] He merely shrugged it off. Amazed, the islanders watched to see if Paul would swell up and die. Their superstitious nature caused them to think he must surely be an evil man to have a deadly snake bite him. When nothing happened, they decided he must be a god.[10]

Paul wasn't God. Paul trusted God.

Paul understood the purposes of God, had the mind of Christ, and in the midst of his greatest trials and temptations, could comfort a panic-stricken crew, or shake a viper into the fire. Paul feared no evil because God was with him.

The purposes of God are going to be served by God, and by God Himself.

We are not the initiators of our salvation, the originators of grace, or the completers of our lives — we are His "workmanship,"[11] who are identified with Him by the blood of Christ, born of His Spirit and His incorruptible Word.

It is God's will that men be saved. It is not His will that any should be lost.[12] He sent His Son into the world to redeem the world so that men should not perish but have everlasting life.[13] God did not send His Son into the world to condemn the world, but that the world through Him might be saved.[14]

If God went to such lengths to deliver us from sin, surely He

45

will go to great lengths to deliver us from all our trials.

Even at this moment as you read this, it makes no difference what you are going through, what your circumstances may be, how you are tempted, the truth is: God is not going to disown you because you have received His nature by the new birth. To disown you would be to disown Himself. That He will not do.

God is working for your good.

Just because you don't feel like you have any faith left doesn't make God dead.

You may blow hot or cold, feel up or down, be optimistic or pessimistic, but God never does.

God will be God no matter what you do.

You can trust Him. You can praise Him.

Your trust during crisis, be it trial or temptation, is not in your abilities, talents, emotions, circumstances, or even yourself — your trust is in the Living God.

In the moment of your need, your trust must be centered in God alone.

God was faithful to Elijah and David.

God never left them nor forsook them.

God would not deny them in their weakness.

God took care of them supernaturally.

God spoke to them.

God renewed them.

God kept them.

Elijah traded a juniper tree for a chariot of fire.

David traded Ziklag for a throne.

God took their weaknesses and gave them His strength.

God will do for you what He did for them.

God will not leave you nor forsake you.

God will not deny you in your trial or temptation.

God is faithful.

Prayer

"Father, in the Name of Jesus, I come to You right now in the midst of my crisis. In the midst of my need, I want to be honest with You. I don't feel anything. I don't sense anything. I can't generate anything. But I want You to know, Lord, that I believe You are my God. I believe Your Word is true. And I believe that right now You are working for my good. Thank You for it.

"Thank You that You will not deny me because You will not deny Yourself. Thank You for Who You are and for who I am in Christ. I trust You totally and completely to bring me out of this situation to a new revelation, a greater ministry, and greater blessing than I have ever known in my life.

"I put my trust in You, Lord. Amen."

Remember

- Decisions determine destiny.
- Decisions made in pressure and fear are degenerative.
- Decisions can take us out of God's will, but not out of God's reach.
- Prayerlessness is often a form of hiding.
- More people miss out with God through impatience than anything else.

- The purposes of God will be served by God and God Himself.

- God went to great lengths to save us, so He will go to great lengths to deliver us from our trials.

- God will do for you what He has done for others; He will take your weaknesses and trade them for His strengths.

PART II
THE CRISIS OF CHANGE

Chapter 5

GOD'S PATTERN FOR CHANGE

Everything God does is according to a pattern and based on a principle. When we learn His patterns and base our faith on His principles, our lives become productive, maximized, and successful. But if we live by personality, theory, and circumstance, our lives will be haphazard, confusing, and driven by every wind of change. One of the main goals for every true Christian is to discover God's patterns and principles through diligent study and application of His Word.

God's Word contains the principles upon which we can base decisions and actions for every situation and issue in life. The Bible is our absolute rule of conduct. If we only want to learn how to respond to certain circumstances, we will never learn enough to cover every situation that can arise. But if we determine to learn God's patterns and principles for life, we will equip ourselves to handle every issue, whether large or small.

We have already established that change is normal to life. One of God's patterns for change is the process of entering and leaving. In a sense, there are only two things you and I ever do in life — enter and leave.

We enter life through birth and leave through death. We leave the womb and enter infancy; leave infancy and enter childhood; leave childhood and enter adolescence and so it goes throughout life. During the course of a day we may leave the house, enter a car; leave the car, enter a restaurant; leave the restaurant, enter the car again; and so on.

As we progress through the stages of life, we leave home, enter school; leave school, enter the work force; leave bachelorhood, enter marriage; leave earth, enter heaven or hell. We can leave one city for another, one job for another, one church for another and, unfortunately, one marriage for another.

Each change comes by way of crisis, small or large. The greater the degree of change, the greater the crisis.

Change accompanies crisis. The process of entering and leaving changes our lives, upsets our routines, and creates new perceptions that can cause us to feel stress.

The corresponding principle to the pattern of entering and leaving can be stated, "How you leave determines how you enter." How we leave one situation in life will determine how we enter the next.

We bring to the new place, city, relationship, job, ministry, or school only what we brought from the old. What is left in our mind and spirit from the old will determine how we enter the new. If we leave with a wounded spirit, unless it is healed, we will enter with the same spirit. If we leave with bitterness, animosity, hostility, unforgiveness, defeat, or fatalism, we will carry those seeds into the place where we enter. Eventually they will sprout and produce the same things we thought we were leaving behind.

Taken in the positive, the seeds we carry for good will produce good wherever we go.

Friends of mine, Roger and Marti, are faithful in their devotion to God. With their church benevolence team, they began going to a barrio twice a month to deliver food and preach the Gospel. This neighborhood was on the "top ten" list for problem areas in the United States. Their first few years there were difficult times of sowing good seed while risking their lives in the den of violence, gang warfare, drug lords, and poverty.

Year in and year out they continued twice monthly to bring food and preach the Gospel. Finally, enough people had heard the

Word of God and believed that they wanted to form a church there in their local language. Roger and Marti's church provided a pastor, and the little fellowship began. Roger and Marti continued to bring food and preach the Gospel to help the little church survive.

Slowly realizing that someone cared for them, the people of the neighborhood began to care for themselves. They petitioned and received government funds to refurbish some of their buildings. Citizens began taking pride in their homes, businesses, and personal appearance. The little church grew. Roger and Marti pressed on, never missing their scheduled Sunday in the barrio.

It has now been seven years since Roger and Marti were called to minister in that area. When they started, they were thrilled when one, six, or ten people responded to the Gospel. Today it is not uncommon for fifty, eighty, a hundred people to be saved in a single service. The area is no longer classified as a ghetto by government standards. And, the local police department has just disbanded its gang unit for lack of gang-related activity in the area.

The seeds of righteousness produce the same effect regardless of where they are sown.

This is why God deals with principles and root causes. The roots will produce the same fruit or result again and again. Circumstances and environment are not root causes. People with the seeds from their experiences and beliefs in their spirits are.

How we leave childhood determines how we enter adolescence.

How we leave single life determines how we enter marriage.

How we leave school determines how we enter the work force.

How we leave a broken relationship determines how we enter the next relationship.

How we leave our place of devotion determines how we enter our place of ministry.

Going Out To Come In

The Apostle Paul taught that temptations and trials are "common to man," but that when they come, God will "make a way to escape."[1] God's escape pattern is never based on an escape *from*, but an escape *to*.

Abram was brought out of Ur of the Chaldees by the Lord.[2] God's purpose in taking him out of Ur was to enable him to enter the Promised Land. Abram left one country in order to enter a better one. Later his name was changed from Abram to Abraham, because of the change in his relationship with God. He left one relationship with God to enter a better one, a new one based on an eternal covenant. God brought him *from* to deliver him *to*.

God delivered His people, the nation of Israel, from Egypt and slavery. His deliverance was not based entirely on where He took them *from*, but where He wanted to take them *to*. The Bible records, "And he brought us *out*..., that he might bring us in, to give us the land which he sware unto our fathers."[3]

So often in times of crisis, we think of escaping from something, some undesirable place or condition. We think in terms of avoiding crises, problems, difficulties, punishment, correction, and the hard issues of life because we are basically negative by nature. God's viewpoint is totally different. Because He is positive, God always thinks of releasing us to something, a better place or condition.

In that sense, crisis is not as negative as the world or our perceptions would have us to believe. Transition is necessary for God to take us out of where we've been and *into* a better place.

God illustrated this graphically when He brought the nation of Israel to the freedom of Canaan. To bring them into the "Promised Land," He first had to lead them out of the bondage of Egypt. To bring them in, He had to take them out.

Those who left Egypt failed to realize what God was doing. *They were content to leave the old, but unprepared to enter the new.* When they saw the land of "milk and honey" which was promised, they refused to accept it as theirs to enter.

Moses sent twelve spies in to see if the land was habitable. Two of them, Joshua and Caleb, came back with a thrilling report of its unproven potential, its raw and primitive nature. The other ten spies were intimidated and afraid. They spread a report about the "giants" who lived there. The nation of Israel as a whole believed the false report that there were formidable enemies which they could not possibly conquer. They were negative in attitude, believed the worst, and suffered the consequences. That generation missed Canaan, and every one of the ten spies died in the wilderness. But God blessed Joshua and Caleb with long life and commissioned them to lead the next generation in entering, conquering, and settling the land.[4]

God gave the Israelites the exodus from Egypt so He could give them the entrance into Canaan. Because the history of Israel serves as an example to us,[5] God's pattern is the same for us today. If we fail to realize that God is bringing us *out* to deliver us *into* a land that is better and brighter than, like the first generation of freed Israelites, we can perish in a wilderness of unbelief. We can miss our "Promised Land" by missing the patterns and principles of God.

God's primary, fundamental goal for our lives is to bring us into a close relationship with Him. God's desire for all His children is Christlikeness.[6] To bring us *into* that likeness and position, He had to first bring us *out* — out of our old habits, wrong attitudes, sinful thoughts, and selfish actions.

We must allow God to lead us out so He can lead us in.

We leave the old and enter the new by way of crisis.

To deliver us *to* salvation, God must deliver us *from* sin. We go by way of crisis. Facing reality, admitting need, humbling

55

ourselves, repenting, are all part of the crisis of salvation. God delivers us *to* righteousness, by delivering us *from* evil.

As God brings us from one level of living into another, the difficult and even traumatic transitions produce stress. The children of Israel failed to realize what God was doing and collapsed under the pressure. They misunderstood God's purpose for leading them out of Egypt. God wanted to take His people to Canaan, the land He had promised to Abraham and his descendants, but all they could see was the wilderness through which they had to pass — the crisis of transition.

We must look beyond the stress of the temporary to the glory of the permanent, from temporal to eternal.

God is more concerned with where we are going than where we have come from.

God always looks at the finished product.

God always looks at the place where He wants His children to be, where He is taking them as they obediently follow Him.

When Elijah walked the earth he experienced trials and struggled with his fivefold temptations. God ministered to him to bring him into a new relationship. Elijah believed that God was a good God, trusted Him, obeyed Him, and traded his ordeal for a greater ministry than ever before. When Elijah left this earth and passed on his mantle, the symbol of his anointing, to Elisha, his ministry was multiplied.[7]

Jesus desires multiplication for us, His disciples. He prayed that we would become one so that the Spirit would come upon us.[8] He knew that we who comprise the Body of Christ in the world would begin to think His thoughts, speak His words, and do His works. In that way, His ministry would be multiplied. But Jesus had to leave and return to His Father in heaven so He could send His Holy Spirit to us, His disciples. God *entered* the world and the lives of His disciples through Jesus Christ, and Christ *left* the world so He could enter His disciples again, this time through His Spirit.

We must be prepared to leave the old so we can enter the new. When we deal with change in a godly way, we will multiply, or increase, rather than decrease.[9]

Leaving our "Egypt," waiting in the wilderness to qualify for the Promised Land, entering Canaan, all create new crises, but each crisis is a step toward a better, higher, more permanent life that God wants to give us.

God always looks at where He wants to take us, not just where we are. That was true with Abraham and Moses, and it is true with us today.

Leaving is necessary to entering; and entering is as important as leaving.

Entering Crisis and Leaving

When Jim called to talk to me about some ministry-related business, the conversation began to include his personal concern with where he was attending church. Jim told me he believed he had been divinely "led" to the church, and he believed he had been sent there for a particular purpose to help the pastor. Now, four years later, he admitted the pastor didn't seem to want his help, his wife was unhappy there, and their children did not want to attend church with them.

However, he was still reluctant to leave because he believed so strongly that God had led him to that place of worship.

"Are you getting ministered to there?" I asked him. "Are you getting any benefit from worshipping there?"

I asked him this because everything in life has the potential of being either a benefit or a detriment.

"No, and neither is my family," he stated emphatically.

"Then why don't you leave?"

"Because God led me there."

"You need to realize," I told him, "that oftentimes God takes us into something so supernaturally that when it comes time to move on, the leaving is so natural we cannot accept it."

Sometimes the entering is so supernatural, signs and wonders follow us as we walk on the path God has for us. So when it is time to leave, it can appear so natural that we miss it. God released the Israelites from Egypt by causing plagues and pestilence in Egypt. That was the exception, not the rule. It was a supernatural act for a specific time in history. *But if we look for God only in the spectacular, we'll miss the Holy Spirit.*

Timing is the essential ingredient in success.

Many people stay longer than they should, creating more problems than if they had left at the right time. That is what happened to Jim. He stayed longer than he should have and developed problems in his personal and family life. He faced difficulties and hardships that were unnecessary.

When I met Jim some months later, he was happy and content. Once he made the decision to leave, and did it right, God was able to take him to the next place He wanted him to be.

When it is time to leave, there will always be those who want you to stay. Their desire will most often be based on personal feelings or sentiment. When God is moving you out of one place to bring you into another, you cannot allow yourself to be deceived into making a decision based on sentiment instead of truth.

Following God's timing will always result in blessing. God can use you at a specific moment of time in a way that is powerful, glorious, and unique.

Success comes when you are the right man, at the right time, at the right place. Timing is the key ingredient.

In the first century, Saul persecuted Christians until Jesus Christ miraculously revealed Himself to Saul and struck him blind. Saul went to the home of Ananias who laid hands on him and prayed for him to receive his sight. Saul's name was changed to Paul. He became a powerful spokesman for the Christian faith, and has spread the Gospel to the present day through the letters he wrote which became part of our Bible.

Ananias was a godly man who rose from obscurity to meet a particular need at a specific time. Then he went back into obscurity, and not another word was heard from him. He entered history and left. His godly lifestyle made it possible for him to minister to Paul and help launch Paul into ministry. He was the right man, at the right time, at the right place.[10]

Success Erases Failure

When you enter a new place, you will have new experiences, friends, and lessons. If you have learned your lessons from the last place you entered, then God will do in you something completely different. If you have not passed the tests God gave you last time, you will do them over again until you have learned your lesson and passed your test. When the Israelites refused to enter Canaan the first time, they went to a place called Kadesh-barnea,[11] and ended up wandering back there twice again before going on to conquer Canaan. We have "Kadesh-barneas" in our lives as well. Those are the situations and conditions which we find ourselves in time and time again until we finally say, "No more! What do You want me to learn, Lord?"

Once you have passed your "Kadesh-barnea" and are entering the new, you will begin new lessons, new experiences, new spiritual growth that you have never known previously. This is God's plan for all growing, maturing Christians. We grow from "glory to glory,"[12] from success to success.

Success erases failure.

There is a God-given pattern for entering a new situation or relationship. You cannot take past experiences and plant them in the fresh soil of a new place or person. You cannot take one friendship and duplicate it with another person, unless you lay the foundation anew. You cannot take the pattern for one business enterprise and imprint it on another business enterprise, unless the new soil is conditioned.

The pattern of the harvest is: Condition the soil, sow the seed, water it, reap the harvest.

Reaping the harvest is the last step, and the most obvious — unless you forget it! Every pastor knows he must make the altar call. Every board member knows he has to submit ideas for a vote. Every parent knows there is a time when the family must stand together in agreement. When those things happen, each in turn reaps the desired harvest.

Any farmer knows that to condition the soil, sow the seed, and water it without reaping any harvest is fruitless and frustrating. The harvest is the purpose of all the effort.

The pattern of the harvest will always work, and work to your benefit.

In the next chapter I will show you ten steps you can take that will enable you to leave and move through transition periods with the least amount of difficulty. If followed, they can bring God's blessing into your life, regardless of what you may be leaving.

Remember

- We are always in the process of entering and leaving.

- The environment of the place where you go will become like the place you left, because you take the seeds for the harvest with you.

- God's escape pattern is not an escape from, but an escape to.

- Transition is necessary for God to take us out and deliver us *into* a better place.

- God's primary, fundamental goal for our lives is to bring us into a close relationship with Him.

- We leave the old and enter the new by way of crisis.

- We must look beyond the stress of the temporary to the glory of the eternal.

- God is more concerned with where we are going than where we have come from.

- God always looks at the finished product.

- Leaving is necessary to entering; and entering is as important as leaving.

- If we look for God only in the spectacular, we will miss the Holy Spirit.

- Timing is the essential ingredient in success: being the right man, at the right time, at the right place.

- The pattern for harvest is: Condition the soil, sow the seed, water it, reap the harvest.

- Success erases failure.

Chapter 6
STEPS TO ENTERING AND LEAVING

There are ten steps in a God-given pattern of entering and leaving that can help pull you through the crisis of change. If you have just left a job, were fired, resigned, left a church or ministry, broke an engagement, started a new career, found the one to marry, moved to another city, started college, or whatever situation you may find yourself in, you can do these steps. Do them in every succeeding stage of your life to help make your adjustments smooth. They are:

1. Realize That Crisis Is Normal

The first thing you need to understand is what we have already stated: *Crisis is normal to life.*

Whenever you are in transition, you will go through a crisis. Crisis is normal in a process of growth. Remember, God's pattern of escape is not primarily an escape *from*, but an escape *to*. God is bringing you *out* of a temporary state to take you *into* a higher, more permanent state of living. Generally, the way from the transient to a more permanent state of being in life is by way of crisis. Keep this divine perspective as you believe on the Lord to guide you through the stages of development.

In the transition, what is in your mind, heart, and spirit is most important to you. *Where* you are is not as important as *who* you are. While God changes the *where*, open yourself to let Him change the *who*. You may leave the old environment and circumstances behind, but remember — you will always take your spirit with you. What is in your spirit will determine what you will find in your new situation and environment.

2. Follow the Lord's Pattern: Forgive

The Lord Jesus Christ is our pattern for entering and leaving. He left heaven to enter earth, then left earth to enter heaven. Each was by way of crisis.

At the cross, Jesus suffered the shame of a criminal's punishment although He lived a sinless life. The extremes He faced while leaving earth to re-enter heaven are impossible for us to comprehend fully. But notice what Jesus did for us. While on the cross, suffering the extremities of crucifixion, He prayed, "Father, forgive them; for they know not what they do."[1] His forgiveness opened heaven to us.

Jesus Christ died on the cross, was laid in a tomb, and rose from the dead — and even though He paid the full price for our salvation, if He had done it without forgiving us of our sins, we would still not be able to enter heaven. The unforgiveness would have barred us from ever joining Him and the Father. His forgiveness opened the way for us.

Life is lived on the basis of relationship, so opening or closing the doors of relationships is as important a pattern as entering and leaving. By forgiveness Jesus opened the door of relationship to Him and the Father.

The same principle holds true for you and me in our actions toward others.

Forgiveness opens, unforgiveness closes.

If you want to open, you must forgive.

Jesus said, "Receive ye the Holy Ghost: Whose soever sins ye remit [forgive], they are remitted [forgiven] unto them; and whose soever sins ye retain [do not forgive], they are retained."[2]

Unforgiveness will cause sins to be retained within yourself. This is true both of sins you commit and sins committed against you. Unforgiveness for either will shut down friendships, associations, and opportunities. When you hold unforgiveness in your heart toward someone, that unforgiveness closes up areas of yourself.

Marriage is a great example of unforgiveness closing a relationship. When a person enters marriage, he or she must leave single life and family. If a man takes his single ways into marriage, he will ruin the marriage. When two people marry, they leave the parents and cleave to one another.[3] By taking their parents into the relationship that primarily is for two, they will end up with his parents and her parents, and try to make a marriage with four people too many.

Spouses who do not forgive their parents eventually find their unforgiveness spoiling their new union. And those whose in-laws are unforgiving will find hardship in relation to their new spouse.

The spirit of unforgiveness is communicated from one person's spirit to others and closes them off. Holding grudges and letting prejudices spoil intimacy is no way to live. It doesn't matter whether it's a wife, husband, child, in-law, friend, neighbor, boss, employee, colleague, father, mother, doctor, or pastor — an unforgiving spirit will close others off and, by doing so, close off part of a person's life.

When you harbor unforgiveness toward others, you cannot effectively witness or minister life to them. Thus you close off heaven to them. But when you forgive and open up that relationship so you can minister God's Word, you have opened heaven to them. Then they can receive Christ as Savior.

Forgiveness is always a gift. Forgiveness can never be earned. It can only be given as is God's forgiveness to us.

Always leave with forgiveness toward everyone and everything. Don't sow the seeds of the past into new fields of relationship.

Once you have left, leave the experiences and opinions of others behind by forgiving all. Whether good or bad, don't try to plant past experiences into the fresh soil of a new place or persons. Even when you experience success in one place, when you change, you start again at the bottom of your new level. Let your new associates get to know you first, then you can share the past with them.

Cause judgments to be based on who you are, not what you were.

3. Admit That God Is Your Source

The next thing you need to do in times of change is to admit that God is your source. Recognize that if you have committed your life to Christ, He — not man — is in control of all you submit and commit to Him.

"The Lord is my helper, and I will not fear what man shall do unto me"[4] is a biblical truth.

Bankers, employers, personnel officers, judges, the corporate structure, or even your church is not your source — God is. These may have authority in your life, and you have to recognize and respect that authority. But there is a Higher Authority to Whom you have submitted, and all these things rest under His Supreme Authority. As your Advocate, He is able to present your case in a winning fashion and win the outcome in your favor. God is the ultimate authority over everything in your life.

I have a great friend whom God launched into missionary service in a powerful way. He became a tremendously successful missionary.

Once he made my house his main office while he was in the United States raising funds to return to the mission field. I noticed something peculiar about him at that time. Whenever the mail came, he would rush to the mailbox to see what was for him. If there was a letter with money, he was happy; if not, he became sad. I noticed that he was depending on that mailbox as his source. The truth is,

God was always working for his highest good, regardless of what came in the mail. He eventually learned that lesson well. If he had not, he would never have been the missionary statesman he became.

Years later I launched into ministry and began to depend on private donations for support. One day I caught myself walking up the driveway from the mailbox, shuffling through letters, and my spirit dropping as I realized there was no income. Suddenly, the image of my missionary friend flashed before my eyes and I realized I was caught in the "mailbox syndrome." I didn't need to depend on that mailbox as my source of supply in my crisis! I needed to depend on God as my source.

Our financial battle is won on our knees, not at the bank. Not at the mailbox. *God is our source!*

Recognize that God is your source, and then never stop honoring Him with your substance. If you are suffering from a financial loss, honor God with what financial resources you do have. Faith operates at all times.

Giving to God is not some kind of super-spiritual bribe that will release you from distress. *You cannot compensate by sacrifice what you lose through disobedience.* You cannot suddenly decide to give sacrificially to God, expecting it to make up for years of disobedience to God. Repent of wrongdoing. Give to God because it is right. Don't try to "buy" or "bribe" God — it won't work!

God is God, and He will do what is best for you according to His infinite wisdom. When we apply our finite understanding and dream up the solution to our crisis, and God does not act in the way we think He should, we can become disappointed in Him. Some are even embittered toward Him. When you give to God, you can expect a return because God will not be a debtor to any man. But when and how He honors your faith is up to God. You may know the biblical principle of the "seed-faith offering." It is valid, but it is not a magic potion. Heaven doesn't operate a lottery. You don't give, then wait to hit the jackpot. Expecting God to instantaneously release us from a lifetime of error is presumption, not faith.

We are disappointed in life not based on what we find, but what we expect to find. When we expect God's blessings to coincide with our decisions, we set ourselves up for disappointment. God's timing is not our timing, and giving is never a magical solution to our problems.

There is a fine line between faith and presumption. That line is the difference between spirit and flesh, grace and works, obedience and assumption.

In short, give your tithes and offerings generously, by faith, believing that God will take care of you, and expect His blessings. But don't give with presumption, presuming you know *how* He'll take care of you or *how* the blessings will come.

Get rid of magical thinking. Deal with reality.

God honors those who honor Him.[5] The greatest way to honor Him is to have faith in Him. Give to God as an act of faith. It is God-honoring. Tithing, like baptism, witnessing, or other acts that honor God, is an external evidence of an internal work. Internally, we have given ourselves over to God. Externally, we die to ourselves and give to Him materially, with our dedication, and with our time and energy, telling others of His Good News. God loves a cheerful giver.[6]

Just as forgiveness opens relationships, so giving opens blessings. Richness in faith will produce richness in life, whether in relationships, finances, or any other area.

God expects us to revere Him as our source. Giving God reverence "adds hours to each day," the proverb says.[7] Reverence for God is revealed in our worship and in our attitude toward worship. Murmuring about the time spent, complaining about how much time God takes out of your Sunday, the Lord's Day, will adversely affect the fulfillment of God's promises — just as murmuring kept Israel from their promised land. When you carefully give God your time, a tithe of your time really, you gain time during the rest of the week. Most men who complain that there is never enough time are guilty of murmuring against the Lord's Day.

Reverence God. He is your source. He is your employer. All your benefits, blessings, and bestowments come from Him!

4. Don't Panic

When fired from a job, preparing for marriage, or in any crisis, you need to ward off the stress that pressures you into panic. Panic and productivity are opposites. Panic is always counterproductive.

The children of Israel in their crisis wavered between two opinions, two religious beliefs. Elijah stood before them and said, "How long halt ye between two opinions? if the Lord be God, follow him: but if Baal, then follow him."[8] They changed from moment to moment, day to day, until God brought them to a place of decision to follow Him.

In the emotional wavering that can vary from moment to moment and day to day, panic can set in with the buildup of tensions, anxieties, and tightness in your spirit that will hurt your ability to think and act wisely.

Athletes call this phenomenon "choking." You "choke" when you tighten up and cannot produce your best due to your emotional, mental, or spiritual conditions. In sports, "choking" causes the double fault in tennis, the missed six-inch putt in golf, and the error in fielding a grounder in baseball.

In spiritual life, tightness and panic blinds the eyes to the Word of God, depresses the spirit, reduces faith, robs the prayer life, and slows receipt of God's answers.

Panic is most obvious when you awaken in the early morning hours, unable to sleep, fearful, mentally searching vainly for answers, being tempted to quit or commit suicide (either social, financial, or physical), and wondering what to do. Then, in desperation, you turn on the bed lamp to read the Bible, but the only thing that leaps out of the page at you are the judgments of

God. Due to your weak state, you apply them to yourself and sink deeper and deeper into depression, unbelief, and worry.

Sometimes this sleeplessness is a very real attack of the enemy of our soul, Satan. David called this the "terror by night."[9] This terror is from a demonic being or the presence of darkness that will try to scare you. It will put a thought in your mind that will jar you from a sound sleep, or speak discouragement to you in your drowsiness that you begin to believe. Psychologists who specialize in sleep disorders recognize "night terrors" as a real phenomenon. They just don't know the cause or cure.

When sleeplessness comes over you by whatever means, get out of bed! Don't just lie there tossing and turning, wallowing in misery. Get up, put on a record or tape that is filled with faith and peaceful music, and let the Word and Spirit of God minister to your spirit, bring peace of mind, and create faith in your heart.

"A relaxed attitude lengthens a man's life," says Proverbs.[10]

David said, "You shall not be afraid of the terror by night, nor of the arrow that flies by day...because you have made the Lord, who is my refuge, even the Most High, your dwelling place, no evil shall befall you, nor shall any plague come near your dwelling."[11]

Turn on some Christian music and tapes of Bible reading, and turn off the television! Don't pollute your mind further with junk from unsanctified minds and talents; instead, renew your mind with the washing of the water of the Word![12] Studies show that television causes greater depression and loneliness, even though those watching it believe it will relieve their depression and loneliness.[13]

Don't panic. Keep productive.

When between jobs, the worst thing for you to do is to sit home all day. It is particularly hard on the wife if she doesn't work outside the home and has to put up with an unhappy and unemployed husband moping around the house all day. That creates strife.

Other family members are not used to having Dad at home either. It may be pleasant at first, but after a short period, his constant presence begins to pall on everyone. The condition is aggravated if the man becomes depressed about not finding work to support his family.

The best thing for a man to do between jobs is to keep the same habitual schedule as when he is working regularly. He should leave the house in the morning and come home in the evening. Keep the living pattern as normal as possible.

5. Admit God's Sovereignty

Admit that fact that God has the sovereign right to your life, and that He can overrule anything and everything in it.

Joseph was sold into slavery by his brothers who hated and despised him because he was favored by both his earthly and heavenly fathers. In Egypt, Joseph was sold as a servant to Potiphar for whom he labored for a time, rising to a position of responsibility in the household. Later, because of his integrity, Joseph was falsely accused by Potiphar's wife and cruelly imprisoned.

Faced with such anger, opposition, betrayal, and injustice, Joseph had every reason to give up and to conclude that God had failed him or even turned against him. Yet even in his times of crisis and confusion, Joseph remained faithful to the Lord. He recognized God's sovereign power and submitted his life to Him in faithful service.

In time, Joseph's diligence and wisdom were recognized and he was promoted from his jail cell to the royal palace. He became second only to Pharaoh himself, and was placed in charge over the entire nation of Egypt. Later he met his brothers who fell down before him, asking his forgiveness for the terrible wrong they had done him. Joseph's response to them was:

"'Don't be afraid of me. Am I God, to judge and punish you? As far as I am concerned, *God turned into good what you meant for*

71

evil, for he brought me to this high position I have today so that I could save the lives of many people.'"[14]

God, by His "Transcendent Glory," is able to take things that are meant for our evil, and turn them around and make them work for our good. God is able to transcend the circumstances of the fallen individual who seems to have no virtue left, nothing to live for, whose mind is depraved, and considered by many to be the "scum of the earth." God can save him, fill him with His Spirit, reconcile him to his family, restore him to business, and make him a good family man, with worth, value, and reputation in the community and benefit to the Church. God's Transcendent Glory can take a man from the guttermost to the uttermost.

God will only work with what we give Him. Give Him all the hurts, rejection, failure, and humiliation, so He can turn them around.

Take your emotions, ambitions, thoughts, and dreams to Him in prayer today, submit them to Him, and He will begin to work them together for your good.[15]

Submit circumstances and situations to God. Let Him take them and do something with them. *God is sovereign.*

6. Don't Limit God

God is a creative God.

The children of Israel limited God. It was one of their problems. They limited God to their human expectations, to what they saw, knew naturally, or experienced in the past. They limited God to their own understanding.[16]

You and I are not our Creator. God is.[17] He is not limited in His nature. God is not limited in Himself, but He is limited in our lives by our faith.[18]

"Tunnel vision" is the inability to see anything to the sides peripherally. Those who suffer from it can see only what is right in front of them. Many times we Christians suffer from "tunnel vision" in regard to God's ability to create. We expect God to work in one way only and end up missing what He is really able to do.

We tend to be limited to what we can see with our physical eyes; to what we have experienced in the past; to what we feel emotionally; to what we have been taught, had preached to us, or read; to our own aspirations; to subjective desires. As a result, we are unable to reach out beyond ourselves in faith to believe God for things that only He can create or bring to pass.

When we pray and ask God to take care of things, then go about trying to fix them ourselves, we limit Him.

When we "cry over spilled milk," and dwell on things that happened in the past, we limit God from working for our highest good in the present.

God is not limited unless we limit Him. *God puts no limits on faith. Faith puts no limits on God.* God can create something out of what seems like nothing.[19]

My favorite example of man's limited vision and God's limitless creativity is something that happened in Pittsburgh years ago. I had gone there during a time of financial depression when there was a 27 percent unemployment rate in that working man's city. My purpose was to teach God's principles to as many men as possible, and encourage them to believe God for His goodness to prevail in their lives.

At the end of the meeting, one of the men in attendance stood to his feet and told us a story that thrilled us all. He said that after working at the steel mill in town for twenty-two years, he was suddenly laid off and found himself out of work. He had always thought he would retire from the mill one day and live off his retirement benefits. But now there was no job, no retirement fund, and his unemployment pay would not last forever. He knew he had to do something.

At home he became depressed and irritable. His tensions permeated the entire home and all those in it. The children "got on his nerves" and he seemed to be always in his wife's way. The first few weeks had seemed like a vacation, but being home all day every day became tedious with nothing to do.

Worse even than the present, the future began to weigh heavily upon him.

"I didn't know about these patterns and principles you're teaching," he said. "I only knew I had to get out of the house and out of the way. So I began to leave each day shortly after the kids went to school and stay gone until they came home. I took long walks to occupy myself when there was no place to look for a job, and I was gone about the same length of time each day that I would normally have been at work. Just like you taught.

"I had been out of work a few months when we had a bad snowstorm. The day after the storm quit I went walking again. As I walked I noticed an elderly neighbor looking out her window at me. When I saw her, I realized she couldn't get out of the house because of the snow, so I asked her if she would like me to shovel the snow for her. She said she would be grateful.

"Later when I had finished shoveling the snow off her sidewalk, she offered me some money, but I told her I didn't want it. The next day when I went out to walk, another widow asked me if I would shovel her walk. I guess the word got out. But I did it for her. When she offered me some money, I took it because she insisted.

"I took that money and bought snow shovels for my sons, and while they were in school I went around seeing if people needed their walks or driveways shoveled. When the boys came home, we all went out and shoveled snow. That week I make more money than if I had worked at the mill.

"It was great. I felt good. We did that all winter.

"Well, when spring came, I went past that same lady's house and when she stopped me to talk, I noticed that her backyard needed to be cleaned. I asked if she wanted it done, and she said she did, and so I cleaned it for her. I cleaned her attic, too, and some of the stuff she wanted thrown away I took home and fixed it up.

"The old adage that 'one man's junk is another's treasure' is true. Some of her 'junk' I sold as 'antiques.'

"I began to go house to house again asking if people needed their yards or attics cleaned, and if they did, my boys and I would do it. That is what started my business for me.

"Now I have my own business and an antique store, and I'm making more money than I ever did at that mill. This winter I'm taking my wife to Florida while someone else runs my business."

He finished by saying, "If I had never been laid off at the mill, I would never be where I am today. When I first found myself without a job, I couldn't understand why God would let that happen to me. When I totally submitted it all to Him, He created a whole new life for me. The best thing that ever happened to me was getting fired. I can praise God for it now."

Yours is a creative God.

Don't limit Him.

Trust Him.

7. Humble Yourself To Obey God

There are some people who cannot admit they are wrong, and others who cannot stand to be wronged. Both have difficulties serving God.

When we are wrong, we must admit it. When we are wronged, there are times when we must fight that wrong, and other times when we must submit to it. Knowing when to fight and when to submit is the key to winning and losing.

Humbling precedes blessing.

"If you will humble yourselves under the mighty hand of

God, in his good time he will lift you up."[20]

If we ask for the blessing but are not willing to humble ourselves, then God will humble us. This is what He did with the children of Israel.[21]

Looking at the great men and women of faith, it is obvious that in each of their lives there came a time of great humbling. Either from a struggle without, or from loss within. But out of that humbling process there came the seeking after God that brought them into new and greater places of ministry and influence.

It is in those most humbling times, those times when we are stripped of everything but our dependence upon God, that we learn to trust and obey Him most. As we learn obedience to Him, we are prepared to reach greater heights than we have ever imagined before. Scripture states that God dwells in a high and lofty place with those who are of a contrite heart and humble spirit.[22]

Jesus left the glory of the Father to enter earth in a most humble way where He made Himself of no reputation and was formed in fashion as a man.[23] When He left earth to enter heaven, He again humbled Himself. He became obedient to the cross so He could again receive the glory He had with the Father from before the foundation of the earth.[24]

Jesus went from glory to glory and overcame all.

The humbling was necessary to the exaltation. *Humbling precedes blessing.*

The pattern never varies. It was our Lord's pattern, and it is ours.

Humble yourself to obey.

8. Trust God To Vindicate You

If dealt with unjustly at the time of leaving, don't return evil for evil. When persecuted, don't seek to retaliate. Rather, pray for those who mistreat you, and trust God for your vindication.[25]

When Moses led the children of Israel out of Egypt, Pharaoh tried to get them back, yet God would not let Pharaoh recapture them. Instead, He destroyed the pursuing army of the Egyptians.

"It is a righteous thing with God to recompense tribulation to them that trouble you"[26] is the Bible's assurance of God's care for you. It's also the reason we leave judgment and vengeance to Him. God will take care of those who trouble you.

"Vengeance is mine; I will repay, saith the Lord."[27]

No matter what happens, God is able to deal justly with our oppressors. If you try to vindicate yourself, you will do so at your own expense. Holding self in check, waiting on God, renews your strength and builds your character. If things are not your fault, hold your peace. Although misjudged and falsely accused and condemned, because He held His peace, Jesus maintained His power and anointing.[28]

When leaving because of a company's bad policies or corrupt methods, or because of a ministry's ineffectiveness, or another person's poor character, don't try to justify yourself by telling everyone else involved where they are wrong. Such actions only hurt you, not them.

Don't vindicate yourself; let your new life be your vindication.

Don't be someone else's scapegoat. If you are blamed for something that is not your fault, take it to the Lord. He will vindicate you. Truth will always win out. God will bring it to light.[29]

If legal action must be taken, do it in a righteous way. Forgive from the heart. Stand on principle. Trust God.

No matter how hurt you are, don't let a root of bitterness spring up in your spirit.[30] Take your innermost feelings to the Lord in prayer.

Let the peace of God rule in your heart.[31] "God is not the author of confusion, but of peace,"[32] says the Apostle Paul. Calm your mind and spirit and let His peace prevail.

On the other hand, be sure your leaving is not something you have caused and then blamed on someone else. "A man may ruin his chances by his own foolishness and then blame it on the Lord!"[33] the Bible says.

Perhaps there has been nothing unjust about your leaving. It is only a company or ministry cutback in personnel or finances, but it has left you without a job, income, or money. Because a man's feeling of security is often tied to his job or profession, a man without money feels as if he has been emasculated, totally deflated. If your leaving has left you in a financial crisis, don't lash out at others because of your dilemma. Remember, your source is God — not your boss, job, or checkbook.

A person who is secure in who he is, and knows his God, acts like it with or without money.

Don't give in to resentment, fear, or depression. You may have lost your job, but you have not lost your sense of worth or your source of wealth.[34] *God is your source of worth and wealth.*

Your heavenly Father has more money in His petty cash fund than the United States has in national debt. He will provide for your needs.[35]

God is truth. He will vindicate you when you walk in truth.

9. Communicate

Don't stop communicating, either with people or with God. Don't cut yourself off by isolating yourself. Loneliness and isolation will only pervert your thinking. Keep your balance by continuing to interact normally while undergoing crisis.

Many people find that when they talk to the Lord in the midst of crisis, they are so tense, they find it difficult to hear from Him. Others have simply never learned to hear from God at all, and stress only makes it worse. If you need to talk, go to your pastor or a godly counselor who is trustworthy and full of the truth of God's Word. If you don't screen those you speak with, and you tell them everything that's in your heart, your "comforters," like those of Job, may seem sympathetic, but often their advice will be based on their own personal perspective or prejudice, not God's truth.

Godly counsel is one of the ways God has of speaking to us. It has the wisdom of God. In seeking counsel, make sure it is godly.

Good advice is not always the same as godly counsel. The Gospel is good news, not good advice. Everyone is willing to give good advice, but when it is not godly counsel it only confuses the issue and clouds the mind.

Outside of such confidential meetings, keep your conversation positive. No one needs to know the negatives of your situation. Though you may be going through emotional turmoil or suffering mental anguish, no one else needs to know the details. We deceive ourselves, and the enemy of our souls takes the advantage, when we think that we must share everything with everyone. That's just not true.

Your children also don't need to know the anxiety, the tension, the anger. Don't communicate to your children the poverty attitude or your brokenness. While for you it is a passing crisis, it can become a lifetime habit for them to overcome. *Knowledge brings responsibility.* Your children do not need to be responsible for the knowledge of what you are going through. If your children are too young to help the family financially, they are too young to gain the knowledge about the financial burdens. If they are old enough to assume some responsibility, speak to them, and get them in agreement with you to the extent that they are capable of acting responsibly. When you are in agreement, in faith with your spouse, you can present to the children a united front that assures them of your authority and the authority of God in the home.

Tell God about your situation — not men.[36]

An old evangelist friend once said, "If I have any confessing to do, I'll confess it to a jackrabbit in the desert and then shoot the jackrabbit." He figured that was better than confessing his feelings to someone who could twist what he said to their own advantage and his embarrassment, or break his confidence.

Be honest with God. Don't be ashamed to tell Him the truth of what is in your heart. Trust Him. Give everything to Him.

Once the negative is all out, immediately get the positive in. The positive is where your strength and God's favor will come from. "No good thing will he withhold from them that walk uprightly."[37] You are committed to what you confess. Confess the positive promises of God's Word, believing them to materialize in your own life, and you will commit yourself to them.

Build your faith through prayer, God's Word, godly counsel, books, teaching tapes, and praise music, then speak positively in every encounter. You may need times of quiet or solitude for prayer and meditation, but with others let your communication be "yea" and "amen."[38]

In short, *communicate everything to God, but only what uplifts to others.*

Faith is believing something you cannot see will happen. Fear is believing something you cannot see will happen. *Faith attracts the positive. Fear attracts the negative.*

Give God the negatives. Don't dwell on them. Take care of them privately. When you want to complain about someone, an injustice or trauma that apparently was caused by a person, take that up with the Lord out in the desert or on a mountaintop. Don't take your murmurings to another person, or live with them inside you. Confess sins, your own and those that others have committed against you, and ask to be cleansed from them. Admit what your conscience convicts you about; don't cover it up.

If you must tell someone how you feel, tell God. He understands and can minister healing to your heart and mind.

Telling others how bad your personal situation is only makes it worse.

There have been times in my own life when I've poured out my aching heart to God while walking the beach, or pushed the shoes out of the closet and climbed in to make my feelings known to the Lord. Sometimes you just have to get alone with God.

Base your conversation on your trust in God, not your trust in your feelings.

God never builds on a negative, but always on a positive.

God inhabits the praises of His people, the Bible says.[39] It does not say that God inhabits gripes, complaints, and criticisms, but that He inhabits praises. In your communication with Him, spill out everything and get to the point of praise. Praise Him out of obedience, and your emotions will eventually catch up. As you give God praises that He can inhabit, God will use your own words to begin to create a new life for you.

10. Act on Principle

Do something!

Do it in faith.

Get your guidance from principles of truth, not from reaction to the feelings of the moment. Act on principles; try not to react to emotions.

God begins all healing with His Word. Spiritual, marital, financial, social, and physical healing all begin with a word from God. God's Word is the basis for everything He does in our lives. Therefore, seek God for the word from Him that will be the basis for faith to believe Him for the solution to your specific need.

The Word of God is sufficient and will work for every need in your life. God will give you a "word" or "words," but it is your responsibility to act on them. This is a little of what His Word says:

"Praise is comely for the upright."[40] To have the presence of God in your life and home, begin to praise Him.

"In every thing give thanks...."[41] Be grateful for what you have. This may also not come easily, especially if things have been taken from you. Turn yourself to the good things that are left and practice thanking God for them.

"Purity is best demonstrated by generosity."[42] Become generous with your time, your prayers, with the Gospel, with your work, your grace, your mercy, your compassion, your money, your talents. As God cleanses your motives and your mind is renewed, the evidence is in your generosity. Spend the time in prayer, then do the work that's there.

God's Word is your blueprint for success. Don't be tossed to and fro by every whim, personality, feeling, or fleeting thought that comes along. Steady yourself in the Word of God.

Remember

- Crisis is normal to life.

- Forgiveness opens, unforgiveness closes.

- Always leave with forgiveness toward everyone and everything. Don't sow the seeds of the past into new fields of relationship.

- Cause judgments to be based on who you are, not what you were.

- God is your source.

- You cannot compensate by sacrifice what you lose through disobedience.

- We are disappointed in life not based on what we find, but what we expect to find.

- Just as forgiveness opens relationships, so giving opens blessings.

- Don't panic. Keep productive.

- Bad things, submitted to God, become good in His hands.

- Don't limit God to your finite understanding.

- God puts no limits on faith. Faith puts no limits on God.

- Humbling precedes blessing.

- God will vindicate you when you walk in truth.

- God is your source of worth and wealth.

- Communicate everything to God, but only what edifies to others.

- Faith attracts the positive. Fear attracts the negative.

Chapter 7
MID-LIFE CRISIS

Perhaps more difficult than leaving a job, city, or relationship is the internal struggle that happens when we leave one stage of life for another. The regrets tend to start, or catch up with us; the pining and yearning to have done things differently can overwhelm.

In a story Jesus told, a rich man had a servant who was a poor steward.[1] The steward was accused of his poor stewardship and was about to be fired. The rich man called the steward in and said, "How is it that I hear this of thee? give an account of thy stewardship; for thou mayest be no longer steward."[2]

In the Bible, there are types and symbols that point out spiritual truths. The wars of the nation of Israel, for example, are physical examples of spiritual truths about spiritual warfare. Jesus' stories are particularly rich in symbolism and types or shadows of meaning. The rich man illustrates God Who will one day call in each of us and ask what we have done with what He gave us.

Like the steward, we are not the owners of anything, we are only stewards of everything we possess. We are stewards of our talents, our time, our jobs, our finances, our marriages, our children, our ministries, to name a few. We must give an account of each of these to God. There are times in our lives when God calls us to account for ourselves, even before the "Great Judgment" after death. Those times may be crises for us.

When we begin to analyze the stewardship of our lives — what we have done with our talents, aspirations, time — we face reality. Typically, we will analyze ourselves when we feel we are getting older. This may be called a "mid-life crisis." The reason people say, "Life begins at forty," is that in our analysis, we realize we are no longer a youth, perhaps no longer a "young married," no longer a "young parent," no longer an intern or apprentice. We see objectively what we have or have not accomplished, and make an intelligent assessment of what we can expect to do with the remainder of our lives, especially if we keep on in the same direction. The approach of "middle life" causes the reflection. The result of reflecting back can be powerful or disastrous.

At such a time, we need to remember that only God has the true perspective. He knows what has really been accomplished, and what we are capable of doing through the rest of our lives. Without His perspective, we'll tend to minimize what we can do. If we do set achievable goals, we'll tend not to break the habits necessary in order to achieve them, and end up defeated and feeling even worse. God can do the impossible in our lives if we'll spend the time to gain His perspective, walk in step with Him, catch His vision, and begin to realize our dreams.

The steward Jesus spoke of realized he was being called "on the carpet." He knew his time at the firm was ending. He desperately needed to do something to make a way for him once his job expired.

"What shall I do?" the steward said to himself. "For my lord taketh away from me the stewardship: I cannot dig; to beg I am ashamed. I am resolved what to do, that, when I am put out of the stewardship, they may receive me into their houses."[3]

Jesus went on with His story: "So he called every one of his lord's debtors unto him, and said unto the first, How much owest thou unto my lord? And he said, An hundred measures of oil. And he said unto him, Take thy bill, and sit down quickly, and write fifty."[4]

The steward went on, making deals with each of the rich man's debtors to reduce their bills. Jesus finished His story saying, "And the lord commended the unjust steward, because he had done wisely: for the children of this world are in their generation wiser than the children of light. And I say unto you, Make to yourselves friends of the mammon of unrighteousness; that, when ye fail, they may receive you into everlasting habitations. He that is faithful in that which is least is faithful also in much: and he that is unjust in the least is unjust also in much. If therefore ye have not been faithful in the unrighteous mammon, who will commit to your trust the true riches? And if ye have not been faithful in that which is another man's, who shall give you that which is your own? No servant can serve two masters: for either he will hate the one, and love the other; or else he will hold to the one, and despise the other. Ye cannot serve God and mammon."[5]

The steward had been an admittedly poor steward. He had not kept the business the way he should have. But he was not poor in spirit or lacking in cunning. There are many principles of the Kingdom of God which Jesus taught us within this short story, but three pertain especially to crisis.

First, the steward knew that life's greatest wealth is not in money, but in friendships. He understood also that "funds come from friends." When our crisis is a downturn in business, economic slump, recession, or worse, the clients, customers, providers, or manufacturers who are friends will continue to do business. Such friends help each other through the rough times.

The steward was not afraid to use money to make friends. He realized that money was not as important as friends were. If he used the money wisely, he would have more friends.

"Never abandon a friend — either yours or your father's. Then you won't need to go to a distant relative for help in your time of need."[6] In this biblical proverb, we see that *distance is never measured by miles, always by affection.* Likewise, riches are never measured by money, always by friends.

Life's greatest poverty is not in riches, but in spirit. Life's greatest wealth is not in money, but in friendships.

Second, the steward showed his wisdom in preparing for what was ahead. "Failure to prepare is preparation for failure," the saying goes. He realized he was leaving a temporary situation and entering a new situation. In the crisis, he kept his wits about him to plan ahead. This symbolizes not just the need to prepare for tomorrow, but the need to prepare for eternal life.

Many times in earthly matters, we prepare ourselves for college, the work place, marriage. Yet often we are ill-prepared for the most important thing of all, our eternal life. What good does it do if we live a "good" life here on earth, but never prepare for eternity? We know we are going to die. "The only thing you can be sure of is death and taxes," is the old adage. To know that, but not prepare for it, is utterly stupid. The most important decision a person will ever make on earth is to decide that Jesus Christ will be Lord of his or her life. The second most important decision is to choose a spouse. Yet how many people spend lifetimes worrying about the second most important decision and miss the first?

Third, the steward knew it was never too late to start over. He was faced with a tough situation, but he prepared himself to leave one profession, start a new career, develop new friendships, and review the means and way in which he lived.

Nothing in life is permanent, not even the state we find ourselves in at middle age. Everything is transient, ever-changing. The only permanence we have is in the Spirit of God and the Word of God. Friends will continue to change, cities will change, businesses will change, and we as individuals will continue to change.

One of the greatest passages in the Bible, repeated often by various writers, is "it came to pass." It's a statement of transition, meaning that something occurred at a particular time. Its meaning is doubly true when we realize things come to "pass," not to "stay." *Nothing that has come to you in life came to stay; it all came to pass.*

I thank God that most of the seasons of my life taught me lessons that have brought me to the present day, but none of those seasons stayed. They all came to "pass." What the relationships, jobs, and experiences taught has stayed within my spirit and personal make-up, but the situations themselves are now behind me.

Nancy and I entered our "mid-life crisis" when God called us individually to account for all that we had done. Even though we had been in ministry for twenty years, God was not finished with us yet! After the crisis of reflecting on our lives, our stewardship, our marriage, our family, our ministry, we submitted it all to the Lord and He made us into something better, more substantial, more beneficial than we had ever dreamed possible.

The ministry we are currently engaged in did not spring from that time of crisis. Instead, we went into a "wilderness," where God taught and tested us for another ten years. At the end of that period, when most people are thinking of retirement, God launched us into a new ministry that is by far the most fulfilling, satisfying, productive season of our lives.

God never starts anything on a negative, and He will never end things on a negative. Anything that is "passing" through your life now will be replaced by something greater, more positive, than what you've experienced before. It doesn't matter if you are fifteen or fifty as you read this, submit all of your past to God, go through your ten steps to leave the past behind, and see what great things He will do with your life!

Remember

- We are not owners of anything, but the stewards of all we possess.

- Distance is never measured by miles, always by affection.

- Life's greatest poverty is not in riches, but in spirit. Life's greatest wealth is not in money, but in friendships.

- Nothing that has come to you in life came to stay; it all came to pass.

- God never starts anything on a negative, and He will never end anything on a negative.

Chapter 8

THE WAY TO VICTORY

"If two of you shall agree on earth as touching any thing that they shall ask, it shall be done for them of my Father which is in heaven."[1]

Agreeing with God releases power in your life. Agreeing in prayer with another person releases faith in both hearts that God will answer. When you stand in agreement with another person, and pray according to God's Word and God's will, there is a movement in the spiritual realm that cannot be denied.

The place of agreement is the place of power.

The place of disagreement is the place of powerlessness.

When the first inhabitants of the earth built a tower in the plain of Shinar, God confused their language to stop them from accomplishing their purpose. Even though they were ungodly, by acting on God's principle of agreement, they could accomplish much. When their languages were confused and they could no longer agree, their plans came to nothing.[2]

In times of transition and crisis, when a husband and wife are in disagreement about what to do, strife always complicates and confuses matters. When there is strife in the home, children react negatively because they are susceptible to the spirit of their parents. Their negative attitudes make the situation even worse. Once a family is in disagreement and the peace is broken in the home, God provides the remedy through Himself and His Word. If the family will come into agreement with God and His Word about their situation, there can be a powerful breakthrough in the lives of all concerned.

"Unite my heart"[3] wrote the psalmist. He knew that "if a house be divided against itself, that house cannot stand."[4] He wanted his heart to be true to God's purposes. Our hearts also must be united so we stand in agreement with ourselves. This means being decided and firm in our commitment to that decision.

Everyone has experienced indecisiveness. When you are undecided, you are easily swayed. But when you make a decision — that the crisis will not last, that Satan will not steal your joy, that your family will not be robbed of God's blessing — and you stand committed to that decision, there is no force in hell that can prevail against you![5]

When a husband and wife are in agreement, the children are subject to their authority. The result of the parents' agreement is authority in the home, as well as peace in the hearts and home. There is power in agreement.[6]

Single people in crisis need to seek a prayer partner or group who will provide a place for agreement in prayer. Two are stronger in agreement than a thousand in disagreement, and a three-stranded cord is not easily broken.[7]

As you stand in agreement with yourself, with God, with others, and press through, *you will prevail.*

Abiding in Christ

When you have entered a new place, or new relationship, you begin a time of abiding. God told Noah to enter the ark, then to leave the ark. But between the two, the Bible says Noah and his family "remained" or "stayed" in the ark.[8]

After leaving, the entering is almost instantaneous. But after entering, there is a period of remaining, staying, or abiding, before leaving.

Jesus talked about abiding that brings the very presence of God into our lives. Through prayer in His Name, according to His Spirit, believers are able to ask rightly, and to see their prayers answered.

It is the abiding between the crises that gives us the strength to endure each crisis. Abiding in God is more important than experiencing a single victory during a time of crisis.

Jesus understood the abiding knowledge of God when He said, "If ye abide in me, and my words abide in you, ye shall ask what ye will, and it shall be done unto you."[9]

Jesus never said, "If you experience Me...."

Experiencing a victory during crisis is great, but abiding in Christ continually is greater. Many people cannot accept this and remain as spiritual "babes," needing the "milk" of the Word, but not taking the "meat."[10] They may continually sin, run to the church altar to pray and repent, then go out to sin again. Far better to learn how to abide in Christ, letting the Spirit of God lead us through each day, away from evil, and into His perfect will for our lives, our "Promised Land" of abundant life.

If we learn to abide in Christ, we learn to live from "glory to glory" instead of from "crisis to crisis." That's the Christlike life.

We need wisdom to live that life. God's Word says, "If any of you lack wisdom, let him ask of God, that giveth to all men liberally, and upbraideth not; and it shall be given him."[11]

It also says: "My son, if thou wilt receive my words, and hide my commandments with thee; so that thou incline thine ear unto wisdom, and apply thine heart to understanding; yea, if thou criest after knowledge, and liftest up thy voice for understanding; if thou seekest her as silver, and searchest for her as for hid treasures; then shalt thou understand the fear of the Lord, and find the knowledge of God. For the Lord giveth wisdom: out of his mouth cometh knowledge and understanding. He layeth up sound wisdom for the righteous: he is a buckler to them that walk uprightly. He keepeth the paths of judgment, and preserveth the way of his saints. Then shalt thou understand righteousness, and judgment, and equity; yea, every good path."[12]

Search for God's knowledge and wisdom, as if you were

searching for a hidden treasure that you were sure was there. We'll give some wisdom for "abiding in Christ" in the next chapters.

The Sun Always Shines

For now, remember that regardless of how dark things may appear to us here on earth, above the clouds the sun is always shining. We know that no matter how dark the clouds, how high the waves, or how strong the winds, above it all the sun always shines. Though we may not see the sun with our natural eyes, yet we know beyond any shadow of doubt that it is there.

The same holds true in the realm of the spirit. Weather affects people, but it doesn't affect the sun. Neither do circumstances affect the Word of God. We don't praise God for the adverse physical circumstances in life, but we do thank and praise Him *in* them, knowing that above it all God is there working for our good. God is *always* working for our good.[13]

Faith lays hold of truth, and truth will always bring freedom.[14]

Know this well:

> *God is for you.*
>
> *God is with you.*
>
> *God is in you.*

Of these three, the greatest knowledge to grasp is that God is in you, both to will and to do of His good pleasure.[15]

His promise is that He will withhold no good thing from those who walk uprightly before Him.[16]

The darker the night — the brighter the light.

Regardless of how thick the clouds may seem, or how violent the storm, the sun is always shining above it all. God's love is always shining bright for you. Submit yourself to Him and to His will for your life, and see where He will take you next!

Let's agree in prayer right now. Pray this prayer with me out loud:

"Father, in the Name of Jesus my Lord, I confess that at this moment You are working for my good. Right now I want to receive these truths into my mind and heart, to walk in them, to trust You to bring me to the place that will bring glory to Your Name. You are taking me out, that You might bring me in. I submit myself to Your care and keeping.

"You are a creative God. I trust You both to create in me a clean heart and to create a better place for me to live. I forgive others and release myself into Your hands. Thank You for what You are doing in my life. I give You all the glory and honor in Jesus' Name. Amen."

Now, confess what God has done for you.

If you would like, write to me personally and tell me what God is doing in your life. I'll rejoice with you.

Remember

- The place of agreement is the place of power. The place of disagreement is the place of powerlessness.

- After entering and before leaving, there is a period of abiding. "Abiding in Christ" between times of crisis gives us the strength to endure.

- Regardless of how severe the storm, the sun always shines.

- Faith lays hold of truth, and truth always brings freedom.

- God is for you. God is with you. God is in you.

PART III

MAINTAINING VICTORIOUS LIVING

Chapter 9

HOW TO MOVE FROM FAILURE TO SUCCESS

When one of God's desires for us is accomplished, when good is done in our lives, in Christian circles the accomplishment is referred to as a "victory." People often pray for "victory," which is a catch-all word meaning the answer to a crisis — whether it be financial, emotional, marital, or any other major issue. Fighting for any "victory" is powerful, God-glorifying, and worthy. Once we win the victory, we need to know the biblical principles to maintain victorious Christian living and abide in Christ continually.

The first principle is, *it is easier to obtain than to maintain*. It is easier to win territory in a war than to govern the territory once the war is over. It is easier to win a person to marriage than to keep the marriage healthy and thriving after the wedding. It is easier to buy a car than to keep the car in good running condition once bought. In every area of life, it is easier to obtain than to maintain.

Some Bible scholars believe that the earth as we know it will end when man's sinfulness influences him to trigger an atomic reaction that causes the elements and atmosphere to catch fire. In the intense heat, the earth will begin to melt, and the minerals will flow out of the mountains in rivers of gold. The seas will evaporate, and the sand will turn to glass. As a result, the entire earth will be pristinely pure, exquisitely beautiful with streets of gold and seas of glass.

Whether the theory proves to be correct or not, the principle behind it is biblical — God's pattern for success is a pattern of purification. God never begins or ends on a negative. God's pattern for creation is to begin on a positive and end on a positive. His pattern for this earth is to start on the positive with Eden, and end on a positive with the New Jerusalem. To end earth on a positive, with all the corruption and pollution here, earth will have to endure the process of purification.

God's plan for us begins with the positive and will end with the positive. We will reach our positive ends through purification. God's pattern for our lives is a pattern of growth. Under His care, we grow, expand, enlarge, and accept greater responsibility.

To grow in God, we must pass His tests of growth, which come through crisis. The crisis does not necessarily make us strong, but shows how strong we are. If we are strong enough to pass, we realize our strength and become even stronger in faith, courage, conviction, and a variety of spiritual attributes.

We can either pass or fail each test. If we fail, we carry that failure with us. *The process of purification purifies us from failure.*

To purify us, God presents us with the same test, and we end up experiencing the same or a similar crisis again. But before God will bring us back to test us a second time, He will cause us to grow. He wants to bring us back ready this time to pass the test, to replace our failure with success, and to move on.

Accepting Responsibility

We must be willing to accept responsibility for failure before we are able to accept responsibility for success. By accepting responsibility for failure, we open ourselves to be tested a second time, which will purify us from the previous failure. We accept responsibility for failure which enables us to accept responsibility for success.

Often men don't want to be put to the test again. But it is only by doing it again that they can become purified from a previous failure.

Many fine church people refuse to leave their pews to start a bus ministry, or go street witnessing, or minister in the nursing home, or teach a Sunday school class — because they don't want the responsibility for having their activities fail. It's the same with those who won't pursue an education, a job, the role of parenthood, and just about any true accomplishment in life.

Conditioned To Succeed

The fear of failure is based on the fear of death. Humans are conditioned to failure. The earth shakes; grass dies; stars fall; businesses collapse; the body decays. Death is a constant threat, as is failure. To overcome failure, we have to be converted to the positive, then reconditioned to think positively.

When we were born, we were born into a selfish society and became like the negative people around us. For most of us, one of our first words was "no." Then we learned "mine." And one self-serving pattern followed another. The Bible tells us that we are converted out of that sin (negative), and into the righteous (positive), when we are converted in our spirits through faith in Jesus Christ.[1]

"So also it is written, 'The first man, Adam, became a living soul.' The last Adam [Jesus] became a life-giving spirit. However, the spiritual is not first, but the natural; then the spiritual. The first man is from the earth, earthy; the second man is from heaven. As is the earthy, so also are those who are earthy, and as is the heavenly, so also are those who are heavenly. And just as we have borne the image of the earthy, we shall also bear the image of the heavenly."[2]

When we are born of Adam, the human, we are born earthy. But when we are born of the life-giving Spirit of God, the divine, we are born spiritual. What is spiritual becomes predominant in our lives instead of what is earthy.

We must be transformed to put us in the positive where we are motivated by faith, by belief, and by success. This is done by the "renewing of the mind" through washing it with the Word of God.[3]

God taught Joshua about success. His statements conditioned Joshua and the Israelites away from the failures of slavery in Egypt, and to the successes of God's planned victories:

"'Only be strong and very courageous; be careful to do according to all the law which Moses My servant commanded you; do not turn from it to the right or to the left, so that you may have success wherever you go. This book of the law shall not depart from your mouth, but you shall meditate on it day and night, so that you may be careful to do according to all that is written in it; for then you will make your way prosperous, and then you will have success.'"[4]

Again, in Psalms God conditioned all of us to succeed in life:

"Blessed is the man who walks not in the counsel of the ungodly...but his delight is in the law of the Lord, and in His law he meditates day and night. He shall be like a tree planted by the rivers of water, that brings forth its fruit in its season, whose leaf also shall not wither; *and whatever he does shall prosper*."[5]

Prosperity is the natural, sequentially-ordered result of righteousness in life.

God's conversion process in our lives takes place at the cross of Jesus Christ, Who is God's Word Incarnate. The cross gives us our victories. Jesus' death was the greatest triumph for mankind. Originally we were created as Adam's children in our flesh. But at the cross, we were recreated by supernatural conversion into God's family as His children.

As new creations, we have recourse to all the resources of heaven made available to us for the totality of our living. We are encouraged by God to go both day and night to use the resources of heaven for whatever our need may be. The total resources of heaven are invested in Calvary, so if we need resources from heaven at any time, we get them through the cross.

Some people feel as though asking God for something in prayer is an imposition on God. They act as if asking for His grace, strength, knowledge, wisdom, ability, is something that will put Him out, will decrease a limited supply. Nothing could be further from the truth.

In our natural bodies, we are subject to the dimensions of time and space. We are compressed, compacted, pressed down, put upon, by these dimensions. We never have enough time. We never have enough space. We live in a world of frustration, inability, and lack. But Jesus is not subject to time or space. As God in the flesh, He took on our finiteness, and when He died and rose from the grave, He gave us the limitlessness of His resurrection life.

God is a God of abundance.

Jesus is not subject to time or space today. We can rely on His timetable and His unlimited ability to do whatever is necessary at any moment to guarantee success. Do we deserve this? No! We deserve death, but thank God, Christ died for us! We don't rely on *our* worthiness, but depend on the *Lord's* worthiness to achieve success.

God loves us unconditionally. Since the only thing outside of Christ we are worthy of is death, it's only by Jesus' worthiness that we have access to the resources of heaven. So whether we feel good or bad doesn't matter. We pray because God tells us to and because He promises that His resources will be there for us when we do.

God's pattern for success for our lives is not based on our ability, because we are limited by our perspective, intelligence, time, space, and our humanity. God's pattern of success is based on the limitlessness of Jesus Christ. When we are in Christ, the limits are taken off.

God's pattern for a Christian's success is the same for each of us, but the individual pattern may be vastly different. Moses went alone to the mount to pray and receive God's pattern for the nation of Israel. When Israel followed God's pattern, the nation was successful. But when they listened to others who led them astray from God's pattern, they went from victorious to vanquished. God has patterns for each of us. No two patterns are necessarily alike.

One of the works of the flesh listed in the Bible is "emulations." (fn: Gal 5:19-21 KJV) *Emulations* can be defined as jealousy to the point of copying. *Emulations* is taking someone else's pattern and trying to make it your own. When you look at the successes of proven men of God, you see they each have their own pattern. Whether it's Abraham or the Apostle Paul, D. L. Moody or Charles Finney, these men received their patterns from God and did not waver or vary. They followed their God-given pattern and achieved monumental success.

Our problem is that we take the pattern someone else wears or follows and imprint it on ourselves, trying to make it work for us as it did for them. We want to copy them. We want to emulate them. But when we don't succeed the way they did, we wonder why. There are similarities that we will have with others, but still our patterns will be uniquely our own.

You can find God's *basic* patterns while listening to a teacher in a crowd. But you will find God's *individual* pattern for your life when you are all alone with Him.

God's pattern for success for you is where you meet Him one to one, and God reveals His will and pattern to you personally.

No matter what may have happened to you in the past, the ultimate goal for your life is not crisis, trouble, or disaster. The ultimate goal for your life is success, holiness, righteousness, and conformity to the image of Jesus Christ.

Remember

- It is easier to obtain than maintain.

- To bring us into success, God has to purify us from failure.

- God's plan for us begins with the positive and will end with the positive.

- We must be willing to accept responsibility for failure before we are able to accept responsibility for success.

- God wants to bring us back to each failed test ready to pass it, to replace our failure with success, and to move on.

- Accepting responsibility for success is based on accepting responsibility for failure.

- To overcome failure, we have to be converted to the positive, then reconditioned to think positively through renewing our minds.

- God's pattern of success is to purify us of past failures, give us fresh revelation from His Word, and lead us in "paths of righteousness" that end in success.

- Prosperity is the natural, sequentially-ordered result of righteousness in life.

- God's pattern of success is based on the limitlessness of Jesus Christ. When we are in Christ, the limits are taken off us.

- God's pattern for success is the same for everyone, but the individual pattern may be vastly different.

- Crisis is not failure. It is only a process.

Chapter 10

THE POWER OF YOUR CONFESSION OF FAITH

"'If anyone publicly acknowledges me as his friend, I will openly acknowledge him as my friend before my Father in heaven. But if anyone publicly denies me, I will openly deny him before my Father in heaven.'"[1]

The principle Jesus was teaching with these words brings an attitude of positive spirituality. This is necessary to maintain positive, Christ-like living. In the *King James Bible*, Jesus' word for *acknowledge* is translated "confess." The confession of Jesus is the rock upon which we stand as Christians. When Peter confessed that Jesus was Lord, Jesus said to him, "...flesh and blood hath not revealed it unto thee, but my Father which is in heaven....and upon this rock I will build my church...."[2]

The Apostle Paul clarified this passage: "If thou shalt confess with thy mouth the Lord Jesus, and shalt believe in thine heart that God hath raised him from the dead, thou shalt be saved. For with the heart man believeth unto righteousness; and with the mouth confession is made unto salvation."[3]

The confession of Christ as Lord is the basis of salvation. It is the rock, or foundation, upon which we build our spiritual lives. Just as Jesus promised, He has built His Church on the rock of those who confess His lordship.

Confessing Jesus is positive. The confession of praise, the confession of gratitude, the confession of forgiveness, the confession of mercy, the confession of providence — all of these confessions are recognition of the presence of God in our lives.

The confession of Jesus is a positive action of faith in God and in Jesus Christ. It is the basis of our Christian walk. Confessing Christ is not the same as soulwinning or testifying, but is used in both. Soulwinning is the deliberate presentation of a revealed pattern of truth. It is presenting Scriptures to lead people to the knowledge of Jesus so they can receive Him as Savior. Testifying is giving a witness to what Christ has done in your life. A testimony is not what leads a person to receive Christ as Savior, although it can be a tool to get him interested. Only the Word will save him. But both are ways in which we confess Christ to others.

When we confess the positive, we charge the atmosphere with the power of God and bring a new attitude to ourselves and those around us. Who wants to be around people who complain all the time? Their words have creative power, and that power fills the atmosphere with the negative. Confessing Christ fills the atmosphere with the positive. We can change the spirit and atmosphere of our home or work place just by confessing Christ.

In prayer, our positive confession of Christ builds our faith. If all we do is confess our weaknesses, we can leave the place of prayer full of sorrow or self-pity. But when we confess out the negative, then confess the reality of Who Jesus is in each situation for which we have prayed, we leave knowing that the power of God has accompanied our confession and that His Spirit is at work in the lives and situations for which we prayed.

Many parents see only the wrong in their children. In prayer, we can ask God to forgive our children. But then we move beyond the sins and into the realm of the supernatural when we begin to confess Christ's forgiveness for them, Christ's care for them, the Father's provision for their salvation, His plans for their lives. Our egos as parents may be hurt to see our children acting up in school or dropping out of church activities, but we have to subject our egos to the Holy Spirit to pray effectively for them.

The flow of God's Spirit is a positive flow, full of the goodness of God, His love, grace, mercy, and forgiveness. When we pray according to His Spirit, or when we confess His goodness during a conversation, we release His power into our lives, the lives of others, and into the very circumstances in which we find ourselves.

Identify With Christ

Confessing Jesus is necessary to being identified with Him. The only way any of us become acceptable to God is through identification with Jesus. It is His righteousness, not our own, that brings us into God's presence. Many people concern themselves with involvement — church, charity, community — while minimizing identification with Christ. Involvement can be "churchianity" instead of Christianity.

At the moment when we confess Christ, we are identified with Him, and He confesses us before the Father. God the Father is pleased with our identification by faith and publicly acknowledges us before men in many ways.[4]

Some came to Jesus and said, "Lord, tell us something so we will know if You are really God or not." But Jesus answered, "Why don't you do what I say? Then you will know if I am God."[5]

If we will do what Christ says and confess Him in obedience to His Word, we will know that He is God because we'll see the results.

Have you ever talked to someone about the Lord and suddenly realized you were saying things that you didn't know you knew? You were expressing truth more clearly than you had ever understood it? That's when the Father was publicly acknowledging you before men. As you identified with Christ, God the Father identified with you; He gave you the "mind of Christ" and the words to say.[6]

We can feel that we're really doing great when we identify with Christ. But what is truly great is that God is willing to identify with His people.[7] *It's far greater for God to be willing to identify with us than for us to be willing to identify with Almighty God.*

109

The confession of faith in Jesus Christ establishes God's work in our lives. Our relationship with Christ and His work in us is confirmed when we confess Him. Confirming God's Word releases His power.

Jesus once healed ten lepers, and they walked away from Him knowing their bodies were completely whole. As they left, one turned around and said "thank You" to Jesus. Jesus answered, "Arise, go thy way; thy faith hath made thee whole."[8] By thanking Jesus, this man confirmed God's work by confessing that Jesus was the One Who had healed him. I personally believe the "wholeness" he received was far more than the bodily healing of the other nine.

Confessing Christ is essential to commitment to Christ. The Bible says that as a man thinks in his heart, so is he.[9] We are what we believe and we are committed to what we confess. When we confess what we believe, we are committed to our beliefs. If we don't confess it, we don't have to admit believing it. If we don't admit believing it, we can change our beliefs.

Jesus was misunderstood and mocked because of His identification with God. He was condemned for claiming to be Who He really was. Often, we can be misunderstood, criticized, and condemned for confessing that we are children of the Living God, that we are joint-heirs with Jesus Christ, that we are a brother or sister to Jesus and part of the family of God. Such accusations stem from Satan, the "accuser of our brethren,"[10] to keep us from confessing who we really are in Christ.

As our elder brother, Jesus offers protection, security, and a high level of living that no earthly brother can provide. Satan wants to confuse that relationship and leave us unprotected, insecure, and low in our self-image. By doing so, he perverts the Gospel. He can keep the Good News from spreading if he can cause us to bottle up our confession and the witness of our lives.

Confession is essential to identification. Confession is essential to commitment. Confession is essential to relationship.

When we identify with Jesus by confessing Him, we align

ourselves with Truth. Jesus said, "I am the way, the truth, and the life."[11] The Way and Life depend upon the Truth. Truth is the core.

Jesus only spoke truth. When He identified with God the Father, He spoke truth. When He confessed that He was the Son of God, He spoke truth. He did not say, "Someday I believe I may become the Son of God." He also did not say, "I am God the Father." He neither understated nor exaggerated when He said simply, "I am the Son of God."[12] This was truth, spoken from a well-defined sense of identity that was grounded in truth. Jesus was secure in the truth. All the devils in hell couldn't shake Him. All the theologians of the world couldn't sway Him.

It is wrong to go beyond the truth, or to speak less than the truth. It is wrong to say we are more than we really are. But it is also wrong to say we are less than we really are — children of the Living God and joint-heirs with Christ. When we claim to be less than we are, we diminish the power of God in our lives.

We are new creations, re-born into Jesus' royal priesthood. If you believe it, confess it. The reason many people are weak in their faith is because they are weak in their confession and identification with Christ.

Lonnie was a fellow I knew who always struggled in his Christian walk. He was constantly coming to me for counsel over the same besetting sins, and never seeing true victory in any area of his life. He seemed incapable of rising above a certain level in his faith before he would experience a huge letdown, become morose and depressed, and come cowering back for reassurance and encouragement. Then one day Lonnie was sitting at lunch with a few friends from work and the subject changed to religion. Lonnie confessed that he believed in Jesus Christ, and identified himself with the Lord. When he went back to work that afternoon, he felt better than normal. He made a point to tell several other people throughout the week that he was a Christian, and each time he felt better. He was actually becoming happy.

Months passed and I saw him only rarely. When we finally got together again, it was not for counsel but so he could tell me about all the changes in his life. As Lonnie learned to confess Christ, he passed that barrier he had always felt, overcame his besetting sins, and became a victorious Christian.

Practice Your Faith

A passage from *The Living Bible* reads: "Don't waste time arguing over foolish ideas and silly myths and legends. Spend your time and energy in the exercise of keeping spiritually fit. Bodily exercise is all right, but spiritual exercise is much more important and is a tonic for all you do. So exercise yourself spiritually and practice being a better Christian, because that will help you not only now in this life, but in the next life too. This is the truth and everyone should accept it."[13]

What does it mean, to practice our faith? Well, what do we mean when we talk about practicing the piano? It means to sit down and rehearse what we know, then learn something we don't know by exercise. Practicing means making mistakes and going over it again. You go over scales repeatedly, and rehearse chords until they are memorized. This is practice.

I've been to churches in my life where a soloist has taken the platform to sing, but it was obvious there had been no practice with the accompanist. Without practice, the so-called ministry becomes depressing and embarrassing for everyone. Who enjoys such a situation? Who wants to listen to a speaker who has not rehearsed his message? Or see a drama troupe that did not take time for rehearsal?

So it is with our faith. We need to practice our faith, study the Word, memorize Scriptures, rehearse what we believe. Instead of listening to the radio or watching television, how much more profitable it would be to practice what you know to be true. We practice confessing Christ in public by confessing Christ in private. Driving down the road, or working around the house or in the yard, we can say out loud, "I believe that Jesus is the Son of God. I believe that He came to earth from heaven, was born of a virgin, lived a sinless life, went about doing good and healing all who were sick and oppressed of the devil, was nailed to a cross, died for my sins, and rose again on the third day...."

This is a confession of Christ and a practice of our faith. Then when we listen to someone, or try to lead a person in the "sinner's prayer," we know what to say because we have practiced it. We know the Scriptures to use to answer their questions. We know what comes next.

At the point of temptation, confessing Christ gives us the power needed to overcome the temptation. The Bible says of the saints in heaven, "They overcame him [Satan] by the blood of the Lamb, and by the word of their testimony...."[14] The blood of the Lamb has already been shed for us, but in order to overcome we need to add the word of our testimony!

We confess Christ in the rehearsing of our faith. We confess what we believe about Jesus, Who He is in our lives, Who He is to our children. We confess Who Christ is to the world, the saved and the unsaved. We confess Christ's power over Satan and the things of this world.

We confess Christ boldly to others because we believe in Him. We grow in grace, faith, and stature with God and man as we confess that Jesus is Lord. This is the power of positive spirituality, the confession of Jesus Christ.

Remember

- Confessing the negative, then the positive, is the key to salvation.

- God the Father is pleased when we confess Christ and publicly acknowledges us before men in many ways.

- Confessing Jesus is necessary to being identified with Him, which is what makes us acceptable to God.

- The confession of faith in Jesus Christ establishes God's work in our lives.

- Confessing Christ is essential to commitment to Christ.

- We have the right to confess that we are new creations, re-born into Jesus' royal priesthood.

- We practice confessing Christ in public by confessing Christ in private.

- When we confess Christ, the Spirit of God will move in us and the power of positive spirituality will begin to work in our lives.

Chapter 11

SPEAKING GOD'S WORDS

God, Creator of the universe, created people to reflect His image. As the reflection of the Creator, all people have His creative power. We are beings created in the image of God. When we put God's Word in our mouth and speak His words, they have creative power in our circumstances. They have power over our lives and enable us to maintain a high level of Christian living.

It is important we understand that we were originally made in God's image and through salvation are recreated in Christ Jesus. One of the differences between us and animals is that animals can procreate, but they have no creative power. Man has a certain measure of God's creative power. Science cannot create, it can only discover what is already created. Researchers discovered the law of gravity and that the world was round. The origin came from God.

But because of the image in which we were created, man has the ability to produce beyond the physical senses. Man's creative power is in the image of God's, which also means His Word. God spoke a word and the worlds which did not exist suddenly existed.[1] Likewise, man is able to influence the outcome of his life with the words that he speaks. Proverbs says that death and life are in the power of the tongue and they that love it shall eat the fruit thereof.[2]

When a man courts a woman, he may find himself in love and desire to marry her. He can fantasize about such a marriage, have all the affection for marriage, and experience the emotional qualities of marriage, yet there is no marriage. But as soon as he says, "Will you marry me?" he has set into motion by the words of his mouth something which will come into existence or die off.

A man can see a vacant lot and think, "What a great place for an apartment building." He can think about the apartments, everything it would take to build them and run them, and yet still that lot will be vacant. But when he turns to a business partner and says, "We can build apartments there," he begins creating something that did not exist. Once he speaks it, he commits himself to the idea, and together they begin exploring its merits. *All the creative force starts with his word.*

Use Jesus' Authority

When Jesus Christ walked the earth, He demonstrated the creative power of speaking God's words. The disciples were at sea with Him once when a fierce storm arose. Panic struck. In their terror, the disciples were thrust into a world charged with fear. They were living at the moment in anxiety, tension, stress, and impending tragedy. When they woke Jesus, Who was sleeping peacefully, to tell Him of the peril, He stepped onto the bow of the boat and spoke a creative word to the storm: "Peace, be still."[3] When Jesus spoke it, the Holy Spirit accomplished it, and there was peace.

Jesus went to a house where a young woman lay dead. He told all the mourners to leave, and He said to the young lady, "Arise."[4] At that moment, life arose where there had been lifelessness. Where there had been the pallor of death, the radiant face of a living soul emerged. His Word created life.

To another person Jesus said, "Arise, go thy way: thy faith hath made thee whole."[5] Jesus spoke, and the Spirit brought each of these things into existence.

Jesus had the Spirit of God without measure.[6] We have God's Spirit with measure. When we "die to the flesh" and allow more of the Spirit to indwell us, we have a greater measure of God's Spirit, but none of us experiences God's Spirit without measure as Jesus did. When Jesus spoke, He spoke by the power of the limitless Holy Spirit within Him. He said and did everything God wanted

Him to say and do, and it was always by the power of the Holy Spirit. He lived in total dependence upon the Spirit.

But Jesus said a peculiar thing. He said, "Greater works than these shall he [ye] do; because I go unto my Father."[7]

Peter understood this delegation of power rather quickly. Days after Jesus had ascended into heaven, Peter went to the temple at the hour of prayer. There he saw a lame man begging, expecting to receive something. Peter said, "Silver and gold have I none; but such as I have give I thee: In the name of Jesus Christ of Nazareth rise up and walk."[8]

Using the Name of Jesus, Peter reached out his hand to the beggar and helped him to his feet. And as the Spirit of God confirmed the word which Peter spoke using Jesus' authority, the man leaped to his feet and began walking and jumping. His legs, lame since birth, were suddenly filled with strength and life.

Use Your Word Power To Create Good

Every word we speak is actually a creative word. We create frivolity. We create sobriety. We create strife. We create ease. Our world is constructed by our words as we saw in Proverbs. Words are potent. They create hurt or health. They create blessing or cursing.

We can speak words of our own and create problems, or speak God's words and create solutions.

We can speak our words and create a hell, or speak God's words and create a heaven.

Jesus said, "'It is the thoughtlife that pollutes. For from within, out of men's hearts, come evil thoughts of lust, theft, murder, adultery, wanting what belongs to others [covetousness], wickedness, deceit, lewdness, envy, slander, pride, and all other folly. All these vile things come from within; they are what pollute [a person] and make [people] unfit for God.'"[9]

117

As men speak words of lewdness, deceit, war, and animosity, they create the world in which these things exist. The secular world as it exists today was recreated by men whose hearts were apart from the Spirit of God. These men were subject to Satanic influence, so when they spoke what was in their hearts, Satan's influence permeated the world. Look at the newspaper. What we see around us is not the world as God created it, but the result of man's influence by the words he speaks.

Your words come from your heart.

Whatever is in a person's heart, whatever is in the thought life, will come out in words. No wonder God says He will call every person to account for every "idle word" spoken.[10]

When the Spirit of Christ is in us, God gives us His thought life through His Word. Reading God's Word is not a contest for time or length. It is taking in the very life of God through His Word. God gives us the "mind of Christ" in and through the Word of God.

As we begin to think God's thoughts, we will begin to speak God's words. As we speak God's words, our world is recreated. It is heavenly! The ingredients of heaven are love, joy, peace, longsuffering, gentleness, goodness, faith, meekness, and temperance. These are also known as the "fruit of the Spirit."[11] These "fruits" within you come out through your words and are reflected in your world.

The Bible says, "When men say, 'Lo, there is the Kingdom of God,' don't go after them. For the Kingdom of God isn't here or there. Behold, the Kingdom of God is within you."[12] By the indwelling of the Spirit of God, the Kingdom of God is within you, and the very Word of God becomes your thought life. The Spirit of God becomes the anointing — the life of God in you.

I was in a situation some years ago where I was terribly hurt by others. God took that hurt and changed it into a new thrust of ministry, making something beautiful out of the ashes of my life, according to His Word.[13] But when I returned a year later to the town where the offense had occurred, I started saying things, making remarks about people who hadn't come to mind since God purged me from the hurt months before. I was losing my peace and joy. Then I realized that I was resurrecting the pain of the situation. I had to control my tongue or else I'd end up speaking words that would revive the entire situation. I knelt down and repented of my words and attitudes. Then I began to confess what God had done for me, how He had purified me from that failure, and my perception of my life began to change.

I was creating an atmosphere absent from God by saying what I wanted to say according to emotions, feelings, ego, jealousies, hurt, and old attitudes. Speaking in obedience to God's thoughts, instead of my own thoughts, changed the situation and restored me to my position of victory.

When God says in His Word that He inhabits the praises of His people,[14] He means literally that. When our hearts overflow with gratitude and thanks to God, we praise Him and fill the air with words and songs, thereby creating an atmosphere in which God's presence is experienced.

Get your heart changed, then let the new words of life flow from you. Negative people will shun you, and positive people will begin to be your friends. They'll bring more positives into your life.

If everyone in the world today repented, received the Spirit of Christ, and began to speak only Spirit-inspired words, our world would change. We would have heaven right here on earth. That's what heaven will be like.

Do you have a need, or does someone you know have a problem? Then pray about what to say, and then say it with the authority of Jesus. Let the Holy Spirit bring healing into your life through speaking the words of Jesus. Jesus gave you the authority to speak His words. You are His mouth, His eyes, His hands, His ears. You are the Body of Christ here on earth. Regardless of who is in need, if the Lord gives you a healing word to speak, then speak it in Christ's stead.

119

Speak words of faith, not fear, and see what God will do!

Live victoriously by being purified from failure, confessing Christ and speaking God's Word. Invest in study of God's Word and prayer to prepare you for your next change or crisis.

You may fail from time to time, but if you'll take these principles to heart, and never quit, you *will* become a winner!

God is the author of your success. Trust Him. Be free in Him. Live free.

Winners are not those who never fail, but those who never quit.

Remember

- Man is created in the image of God, with a measure of God's creative power in his word.

- We influence the outcome of our lives with the words we speak. Our world is constructed by our words. Words are potent.

- As you begin to think God's thoughts, you will begin to speak God's words. As you speak God's words, your life is changed into a place worthy of the Living God.

- Change your heart, change your words, change your world.